Silent No More

Silent
No More

*Victim 1's Fight for Justice
Against Jerry Sandusky*

Aaron Fisher
Michael Gillum, M.A.
Dawn Daniels
with Stephanie Gertler

BALLANTINE BOOKS
NEW YORK

Published in the United States by Ballantine Books,
an imprint of The Random House Publishing Group,
a division of Random House, Inc., New York.

BALLANTINE and colophon are registered trademarks
of Random House, Inc.

All photos courtesy of Dawn Daniels

ISBN 978-0-345-54416-2
eBOOK ISBN 978-0-345-54417-9

Printed in the United States of America on acid-free paper

www.ballantinebooks.com

246897531

FIRST EDITION

To those who serve and protect.

*And to children everywhere
who have suffered and overcome—
and those who are still determined to heal.*

The world is a dangerous place, not because of those who do evil, but because of those who look on and do nothing.

—ALBERT EINSTEIN

Contents

Introduction

Conviction

Aaron

THERE ARE SOME DAYS AND NIGHTS THAT STICK IN MY HEAD AND others that I've been trying to push away for about six years now. One that sticks is Friday, June 22, 2012. The Jerry Sandusky trial had ended just the day before. Even though I should have been feeling a sense of relief that it was over, I knew the jury was still out. I also knew I'd been lied to and disappointed so many times before that I couldn't believe anything good would come of anything ever again.

Part of me thought that I should have stayed home that night with my mom and waited for the news, but I had just started my first real job, as a security guard. The company had me working the graveyard shift that night, which is what you do when you first start out. No one knew who I was. Well, let me put it this way—they knew my name but they didn't know my story. I couldn't give them the real excuse that I was waiting for a verdict to come in and that's why I couldn't show that night. I had a responsibility to the company. I also had to get out of the house because I couldn't take the waiting.

Around ten o'clock, I headed off to work. Before I got in my car, I checked the backseat and the trunk the way I always do. Since all this started I always make sure that no one and nothing is in the car that shouldn't be there. I have this heightened sense of alertness.

Like I said, part of me wanted to wait with my mom but I figured that juries don't come back that late at night anyway. I pictured those jurors sitting in a room, trying to decide and then saying they might as well just go back to their hotel because they weren't sure whether to vote guilty or not guilty. Besides, the trial had ended just the day before.

I thought about my mom sitting by the phone and glued to the TV; I knew that my psychologist, Mike Gillum, was at home and probably doing the same. It was better to just be on the open road that night. When I got to the job site, I knew, I'd be by myself, pretty much out in the middle of nowhere, which was a good place for me to feel safe. I also liked that people relied on me for protection. I made sure there was no one trespassing and no break-ins and no fire hazards. I liked knowing that I was the one who could check the area with my flashlight and check the locks on the gate and make sure that everything was the way it should be so that everyone was safe.

Being alone and awake through the night was a familiar thing. For the last six years, and for sure the last three, all I did was think, and thinking kept me up all night long. Working the graveyard shift was perfect since being awake came easy for me. When I was awake, I couldn't have nightmares.

I was cruising along the highway when my cellphone rang. It was Mom. I figured she was just checking up on me but when I heard her voice I knew something was up. At first I got real scared because she was crying. I was afraid to hear what she had to say. Then she said that Jerry was convicted. The jury had found Jerry Sandusky guilty on forty-five counts of sexual abuse.

I didn't pump my fist in the air or let out a cheer. Instead, I pulled my car onto the shoulder of the highway. I couldn't see the road in front of me anymore through the tears. I just put my head down on the steering wheel and cried. Happy tears, but I was crying.

Nine of Sandusky's victims testified at the trial. No one had a name—just a number. My name is Aaron. I am the boy they used to call Victim 1.

Part One

The Crime

1

What I Wish
I'd Known Then

Dawn

LOOKING BACK, IT WAS ALL RIGHT THERE IN FRONT OF ME. I BEAT myself up every day. None of what happened to my child is behind me, nor will it ever be. Think about when your kid falls down and scrapes his knee. You figure that you should have been closer behind so you could have caught him. Or maybe you should have made sure he was wearing different shoes, or should have tied his laces better. As a mother, when something bad happens to your child, you blame yourself.

I still lie awake at night while the questions haunt me. How could I not have known? How could I not have seen the signs? Was I really that blind? Was I so stupid that I didn't figure it all out sooner? I am not a stupid woman. I tell myself that I was up against a man far more powerful than me, but it's still no excuse in my mind. There are some who understand. I also know there are people who blame me. I read the blogs and websites with all of their comments. One person said I was far from mother of the year. Another said I let my little boy go to an old man's house so that I could party.

Here's the thing: I did not let my child go with a stranger. I let my child go with someone who was a "pillar of the community."

Someone whom everyone worshipped and thought was every kid's savior. Those people who call me names and condemn me? I think to myself, if you people only knew how I was fooled. If you only knew how Jerry made himself a part of our family. I met his wife. I played with his dog. But above all I trusted him, and one of the reasons I trusted him was that everyone else did, too. He founded the Second Mile, which billed itself as a charity camp for children who need direction and hope. How was I supposed to know?

I still have no place for the guilt. I have nightmares now where I can see that basement room where Jerry Sandusky had my child. Even now as Sandusky sits in jail, my guilt is relentless. I didn't think something like this could happen in a million years. Not with a guy like Sandusky. Maybe it was something that I didn't want to believe, because we often don't see what we don't want to believe. What Jerry did to my son will remain unforgivable, but I have a hard time forgiving myself, too. But then, this is not about me. This is about my son.

I'm thirty-six years old and the mother of three children. Aaron is eighteen, Katie is fourteen, and Bubby is eleven. Lately, I am known more as Aaron's mother because he had the courage to come forward. He now has the title of Jerry Sandusky's Victim 1 and I wish that had never been his fate. I am proud of his courage but I wish that he never had to be looked upon as a hero for something like this.

I've spent the better part of my life trying to take care of my kids, which isn't easy when you're on your own. I'm lucky to have my parents, a sister, and friends whom I can depend on and trust. The problem is that now I don't trust people the way I used to. I never will again.

When I got pregnant with Aaron, I was seventeen and lived in Daytona Beach, Florida, with Aaron's father, Michael. We were childhood sweethearts from high school and ran off together. It was like the movies. We were the couple who drove around town in his Mustang with the radio playing. One time, when Michael was teaching me how to drive, I wrecked that Mustang and crashed it so bad that my skull was fractured. I have the scars to show for it. After my injuries healed, we just took off. Crazy kids, I guess.

Michael and I had a way of living that was all well and good when we were kids, but once I got pregnant, I grew up real quick—much faster than I'd planned on. When I was three months pregnant, something kicked in and I just knew then that Michael wasn't the kind of person I could raise a child with. I moved back home to Lock Haven, Pennsylvania, with my mom and dad.

Lock Haven is a small town, and most of the people either know you or know someone who knows you, and those of us who've stayed there have known one another since we were kids. The town has about ten thousand people and it's only about three square miles. My older sister still lives in the area with her husband. They don't have kids and won't have kids and they have a good life. We're close in the way that sisters are close when their lives are different. My parents are just a few miles away in the next town. I have roots here and so do my kids.

So, there I was, pregnant with my baby, when I met a guy named Cliff, who wasn't from town. He worked construction in the area but he was from Kentucky. When you're eighteen, single, and pregnant, life is not easy. Cliff swept me off my feet and didn't seem to mind when I had the baby six months later. Aaron and I moved with him to Johnsonburg, Pennsylvania, where he got a job at the paper mill. Johnsonburg is only about a ninety-minute drive from Lock Haven, so Cliff and I came back every weekend with Aaron and spent time with my folks. He was getting divorced and had two kids, so he wasn't a stranger to babies. He was a good guy and I felt like I was beginning a decent life for myself and my son.

One day, when Aaron was about three months old, Michael drove up to our house in Johnsonburg. Somehow he had found us. It was around ten o'clock at night and he said that he wanted to have a look at the baby. He said "the" baby, not "his" baby. I had always told him that he could see his boy, and I had no intention of keeping him from his son or keeping his son from him. Michael just looked at Aaron. He didn't touch him or hold him or anything. He just looked at him and said he looked just fine and then he drove away.

The next time Michael saw Aaron, Aaron was almost a year old. I'd taken him to visit with his paternal grandmother in Maryland. We were at a mall in Columbia and I took him on the carousel, which, I was surprised to find, Michael was working at. I don't think even Michael's mother knew he was working there. Michael wasn't at all interested in Aaron. His mother took some pictures of Aaron and me, and then we left and Aaron hasn't seen his father since.

I've always been honest with Aaron about his father. I've told him about things that his father and I did together and all the fun times we had, and I never said anything bad about Michael to him. I've even offered to take him to see his father if he ever wanted to. Right around the time Jerry was arrested, Michael went to jail. I found that out right before the Sandusky trial started and I didn't hide it from Aaron. I showed Aaron his father's picture on the Internet and he read the news story about the case. I just think that it's always better to know the truth. The truth that his father was in jail was hard on Aaron, especially given the nature of the crime: On Michael's mugshot, it clearly stated that Michael is a registered sex offender.

Now, Cliff and I never did get married, although we came close. We were together until Aaron was almost five. We got a house and lived in Tennessee for a bit, and then we lived in West Virginia for a while. When we lived in West Virginia, Aaron was just over a year old and my parents were missing him. They started asking if they could take him for a weekend here and there, so we'd meet halfway and do the baby swap. I knew it was great for them and for Aaron, but every time I handed him over to my parents, I'd drive away feeling empty-handed and start to cry. It started out with Aaron just spending weekends with my folks, and then it grew to a weekend plus part of the week. If the time between visits got any longer, my parents would say how it had been a month since they'd seen him, so when were they going to get him again? We'd meet at a steakhouse in Staunton, Virginia, have dinner, and swap out again. During those times when Aaron was with my folks, I worked with Cliff. When Aaron was back home with me, I stayed at home with him.

I started out as a fire watch, and when Cliff and I were in West Virginia we worked as a welding team. I'd gotten my certification because Cliff always said that girls make better welders than guys; he said they're steadier with their hands. I also worked in construction and at a plant where they made wood chips. Cliff and I were often alone in the plant at night and for fun we'd race Bobcat loaders around in the fields. We were still really kids, even though we both had kids of our own, and we were having a great time. It was good knowing that my baby was safe and happy with my parents.

Cliff's older brother and his wife drove a semi truck and we traveled all over the place with them, hitting all of the amusement parks along the way. We drove as far as California, and during the O. J. Simpson trial we even got thrown off Nicole Brown Simpson's property as we snooped around. We went to Disneyland and Magic Mountain and Six Flags and toured Los Angeles. One time when we were back east, we took a picture of Aaron at the wheel of the semi. He was about three.

Cliff and I decided it was time to get married and settle down. His divorce was final, so we started making plans for a really big wedding. I picked out a wedding dress and chose the kind of flowers I wanted and even rented a gazebo. We were living back in Tennessee at the time and I had made one really good friend. Cliff's brother and his wife owned a restaurant in town and my friend managed it when they were on the road. Well, I thought that she was my friend, until Cliff confessed that something had happened between him and her. I was devastated. Our wedding was just a couple of months away.

I wanted to go home to my parents and my baby, and I tried to leave for the next three weeks, but Cliff kept stopping me. One time he even took the tires off my car. In the meantime, my parents didn't know what was happening with Cliff and me. They just thought that I was planning my wedding and that's why I seemed stressed out. I was afraid that if I told them what Cliff had done, they'd hate him forever—and what if I changed my mind and forgave him? They had Aaron with them and I was glad, because I didn't want Aaron around while this whole mess was going on. Finally, I just went home and told my parents that Cliff had to work out of town for six months and so we had postponed the wedding. Leaving Cliff was one of the hardest things I ever did in my life, but I knew that I could never trust him again. Eventually I told my parents the truth.

Once I was back in Lock Haven, I met Eric. I'd actually known Eric for most of my life, so it's more accurate to say that I met him again. He's about six years older than me, and had been in the same class as my sister. I remembered when we were kids and all used to hang out at my grandparents' house. We laughed about the time when they were in elementary school and he tried to kiss my sister; she kicked him with her wooden clog.

It was easy being with Eric. Even though we didn't really know each other, we had a lot of the same friends and we had this shared history. We weren't together six months when we got married and I was pregnant with my second child, Katie. Then we had Eric Jr. four years later. Eric Jr. hates being a junior so we've always called him Bubby.

Eric and I were married for five years, but he began to abuse me when Katie was a baby. Eric turned out to be very controlling and he was emotionally *and* physically abusive.

Aaron at eight years old

Eric worked out of town. He started out working as a technician for a computer company, and then he installed cable for a cable contractor. Often when he came home, I sent Aaron to my parents' house. Above all, I wanted to protect Aaron. One time he pushed Aaron, who then fell over a baby gate that blocked our stairs. Also, I didn't want Aaron to see Eric beating on me. Then there came a time when Eric hit Katie and I made him get out. Katie was diagnosed as bipolar when she was a little girl. Since Eric beat her, she suffers from post-traumatic stress as well.

After Eric and I divorced, I took my three kids and three baskets of laundry and moved back in with my folks in Lock Haven. At last, I realized that I needed to grow up and really take charge of my life.

I might have been just a kid myself when I had Aaron, but it doesn't excuse anything that happened. I had been in an abusive marriage and gotten out of it. Now I needed to give my children the best life possible. I could no longer allow any men into my life who could end up hurting me or my kids.

It chills me even now to realize that the worst still lay ahead.

After Eric and I split up, I sometimes worked for a call agency in town, selling magazine subscriptions over the phone. I put Katie in the preschool program at Head Start and put Bubby in another day facility for infants. I was working thirty hours a week but it didn't last long, because the day-care costs for Bubby were more than I could earn. I'm not a firm believer in day care when it comes to infants anyway. Babies can't tell you if something is wrong. My parents helped me with the kids, but I couldn't expect them to take care of all three of them. So I got some assistance from the state and moved into public housing after living with my parents for about four or five months. I even got my GED and enrolled in college at Kaplan University. I was still in college when all of this stuff broke with Aaron, so I had to put my education on a back burner.

Aaron was about ten and a half and in the fourth grade at

McGhee Elementary School when Nancy Bruckner, the guidance counselor, called me. Nancy knew that I had come out of an abusive marriage and that the divorce had just been finalized. She knew because it's a small town and because I had to file for a restraining order, called a PFA—Protection from Abuse. The school put it on the record that there had been domestic violence. I was a single parent now, and the school had to have a heads-up about the situation in case there were any issues with Aaron at school or if Eric tried to show up there.

As I said, Nancy was aware of what the kids and I had been through, and she said there was a program that would be beneficial for Aaron. She told me a little bit about the Second Mile and their summer camp on the grounds of Penn State. Nancy said that each school district only got to refer a couple of kids, and since Aaron was such a good kid and a good athlete, and especially because there was no father in the picture, this was a perfect fit for him.

I'd never heard anything about the Second Mile before, but after Nancy told me all about it and I filled out the forms, it sounded great. It felt like a good opportunity for Aaron, who would otherwise just have been hanging out with his friends and playing catch and riding his bike around the yards. This was a chance for him to have a one-week sleepaway camp. That was something I couldn't give him for sure.

I drove him up to the Second Mile camp in the town of State College, where Penn State is located. It was the summer after Aaron finished fourth grade. He was pretty excited but a little hesitant, because he didn't know any of the other boys there. I was a little nervous, too, because I'd never been away from him unless he was with my folks.

We had to register at a big building, where they did a bunch of safety and medical checks, including combing the kids for lice and making sure they had all their shots and the supplies they needed. I was beginning to feel a lot better about the place. It seemed like they took real good care of these kids; there was swimming and all kinds of other sports, as well as team-building exercises. It seemed golden and I trusted the place.

The next summer, Aaron couldn't wait to get back to camp at the Second Mile for another week. That second summer, just like the first, they had a closing ceremony. But at this year's ceremony I met Jerry Sandusky. Aaron really wanted me to meet him. I remember how excited Aaron was. He was eleven and a half years old.

"You have to meet this guy, Mom. It's Jerry Sandusky!"

I said, "Who is he?"

To this day I'm not big on football, and I'd never heard of the guy. I saw him talking to people who seemed to know him but I didn't think much of it. Even when he was speaking at the ceremony, I figured he was just one of the speakers and there were a few of them. When Aaron introduced us, Jerry shook my hand, put his arm around Aaron, roughed up his hair, and said, "You got a good kid on your hands there." I thanked him and said that I thought Aaron was awesome, too. Then Jerry said he hoped we had enjoyed the camp and to please come back next year. He went on his way and that was it that day.

Just a couple of weeks later, after camp ended that second summer, Jerry called my house. It was July. He asked if we wanted tickets for the Penn State/Akron game and then he said that he was taking some area kids to Blanchard Dam to swim and maybe even do some Jet-Skiing. Would it be okay for Aaron to go, too? He said that he would transport them and pick them all up, so I didn't have to worry about driving. I asked how many kids were going and he named a few; Jerry said that Aaron should know them from camp.

I was a little hesitant. It was Aaron's first time going off with someone who I really didn't know. In the meantime, of course, after Jerry called and asked me for permission, I called some friends to see what they thought of the idea, then I called my dad and I said that this guy Jerry Sandusky from the Second Mile had asked to take Aaron on a day trip; what do you think? When my dad heard, he said, "Wow! Jerry Sandusky!" When I mentioned it to some of my neighbors before Jerry came to pick up Aaron, they all said, "Jerry Sandusky is coming to your *house?*"

When Jerry came to pick up Aaron, everyone was watching from their windows. All the neighbors were talking and buzzing, and it was only then that it occurred to me just what a big figure he must be. I really didn't know anything about him but everyone else seemed to know. Until then, I had no clue. Little by little, I was beginning to realize that this Sandusky guy was a big deal.

After Aaron went off with Jerry and two other boys to Blanchard Dam that day, I was talking to my dad. He said that when he was president of the local baseball league and my mom ran the concession stand, he knew who Jerry Sandusky was because there was another little boy that Jerry used to hang out with. My dad actually knew the boy because he played on the same ball team as me when I was twelve. My dad said that Jerry used to run around with that boy all the time and he once heard that Jerry even paid for the kid's college education. I figured my dad thought Jerry might do the same for Aaron one day.

I never thought about sexual abuse when I wondered if Aaron should go to the dam that day with Jerry. I only asked my friends and my dad about Aaron going off with this Jerry Sandusky because I didn't know him well, even though he was one of the bosses at the camp. I was cautious about people I didn't know. I actually checked out guys I dated to make sure that they had no criminal records, or even to see how many traffic tickets they had. But I still wasn't worried about Jerry Sandusky when it came to stuff like that. Jerry Sandusky was squeaky clean, and even if I had looked him up, there wouldn't have been anything there. As we all learned once it was too late for my child, Jerry had been getting away with his abuse for years.

If there are lessons to be learned from all of this, one is certainly that if you have a gut feeling about anything like this, never mind who the offender might be—listen to your heart. It doesn't matter whether you suspect a teacher, a politician, a coach, or any of those people who are called pillars of the community.

The other lesson I learned is to push your child to talk. And if he or she doesn't open up, then make them talk to someone else. Forbid your child to see the person who gives you the feeling that something is not right. I know now how wrong I was, but at the time I believed that my child would tell me anything and everything.

I also believed that Jerry Sandusky was some sort of an angel.

2

Meeting the Monster

Aaron

WHEN I GOT TO THE SECOND MILE CAMP THAT FIRST SUMMER, I'D never been on the campus of Penn State before. It was awesome. All of us campers walked into this building that looked like an armory and we all set down our stuff. There were quite a few of us boys there. I didn't know any of them, but we were all the same age, from all over the counties. There were maybe a hundred of us. I knew I'd be there for a few days, and even though I didn't know what I was going to be doing, I was happy to just be there and I couldn't wait to check it out.

We were in groups for sports and arts and crafts and we played a lot of games—including dodgeball, which I really liked a lot. It was a real summer sleepaway camp, even though it only lasted seven days. Jerry formally introduced himself to all of us that first summer, but we all knew who he was. A pretty famous coach and the guy who started the Second Mile and ran the place. He was the boss.

That first summer, after I got back home, I just hung out with my two best friends. We went biking around town and playing ball and swimming. One of my friends had a pool at his house, which was great, but sometimes we went to the lake beach down by the YMCA. It was just another one of those lazy summers. Maybe you've seen summers like that in movies, where in towns like mine you can leave your house in the morning and come back just before the sun sets; where there's just nothing better than summer and no one worries about where you are. Nothing bad ever happened in my town, so kids could be running around and biking all day long.

If anyone had told me then that my first summer after the Second Mile camp would be the last of my childhood, I never would have believed them.

When I went back to the Second Mile the next summer, Jerry introduced himself to all the groups again, but he more personally introduced himself to me. He hung out with my group more than others, which was pretty cool. It was also cool not to be the new kid anymore and to know the ropes. Jerry was doing his usual mingling from group to group but when we were playing games, he seemed to notice me more than the other kids. He said how well I was doing in the games and that I was real competitive.

There were about fifteen or twenty kids in my group, so I was happy that Jerry took a shine to me. He'd rough up my hair and cheer me on and once he pulled me aside and asked me a lot of questions about the camp—what I would like to have more of and if I liked it and how he could make it better. I said that I liked the sports and dodgeball most of all, and he said that the next summer we'd play more of that. He even decided to feature me and my sister in the camp's promotional videos that summer—with Mom's permission.

A few weeks after that second summer of camp, Jerry called my mom to say hi and ask if she wanted some football tickets. Then he asked if he could take me and some other kids for a day trip to Blanchard Dam.

I look back now and understand from my sessions with Mike Gillum that Jerry had things all planned out from the start. It's

Aaron at twelve, nearly two years
after meeting Sandusky

taken me all these years to realize that I was too young and innocent to know what was happening—or was about to happen. I was eleven and a half that second summer. How was I supposed to know that he had a big plan for me then? Looking back, I can put two and two together. Back then, I couldn't. I wish I had. I want other little kids to see the signs that I didn't.

People keep saying that Jerry took an interest in me because I was fatherless and because I didn't have a strong male figure in my life. I did have a stepdad once, and that didn't go so well. The male friends and boyfriends that my mom had in her life had no effect on me, either positive or negative. I was a grandparents' kid. My grandparents always had me over at their place and bought me things. My grandfather—I call him Pap—had been in my life from the time I was a baby. I wasn't looking for a father figure—I had one in him. So when Jerry was paying so much attention to me, I wasn't thinking, "Wow, this is great. I finally have some kind of a dad paying attention to me." I just thought it was cool that Jerry was asking me my opinion on stuff at the camp and that he thought I was a good athlete. I started to feel real lucky and proud that I was Jerry's favorite kid at camp.

When Jerry picked me up that day for the trip to Blanchard Dam, Mom walked me out to his car, which was parked outside our apartment. There were other kids there: one in the front seat and one in the backseat. Jerry sat behind the wheel of his silver Honda in a T-shirt. When Mom saw the other kids she seemed more relaxed, and I was glad because I knew that she was worried at first. I climbed into the backseat and it was like we were off for an adventure.

Blanchard Dam is located in Bald Eagle State Park, which isn't far from State College. The park is just acres and acres of land, and the drive was long enough that it felt like we were all taking a fun road trip. When we got to the park, we played in the playground and did some water games in the lake. Jerry had even brought stuff for a picnic; we had snacks and drinks and sat around the picnic tables. It was just a typical perfect summer day—not too hot—as we sat outside just talking and laughing and having a good time. There were no funny feelings that day. No nothing at all. We were all together—just the three of us boys and Jerry.

Even though I look back and realize now what I didn't know was happening then, I still can't say I felt singled out that day. It wasn't like it had been at camp when Jerry was cheering me on so much. There was nothing in my mind that made me question why Jerry wanted to be with me or with any of us kids that day. To me, he was just a really good guy who ran a camp for kids and did things with them. In my almost twelve-year-old mind, there was no wondering why he wanted to hang out with kids since he was a grown-up. I just thought he was generous. I had no reservations and no suspicions. I didn't get any negative feelings. I just thought, Man, this is a great day.

That was really the only thing that Jerry and I did that second summer. But then in the fall, Jerry started picking me up with other kids and we started going to this hotel near the Penn State campus where they let Jerry use the indoor pool even though he wasn't a guest. But one day at the pool, when there were about four of us boys there, I got my first sort of funny feeling. Jerry was roughhousing with all of us in the water, but when he picked me up—you know, to toss me in the air and then I'd come down with a splash—I felt like he was holding on to my crotch just a little too long. I was wondering if the other kids felt that way, too, but I would never have asked them something like that. I told myself that I was just being stupid and we were all just playing and it was probably just my imagination anyway. I felt very awkward but decided not to think about it.

After that, Jerry started taking a few of us places, and I was the kid who always got to ride up front with him. After a while, he drove with his hand on my thigh, and it creeped me out a little. But then I told myself that this was probably just Jerry's way of being affectionate with me. I figured that's just what Jerry does, the way he is with kids, even though it made me feel weird. Also, I was taught that if I go over to a friend's house or to anyone's house, for that matter, I should respect the adults, the rules, and whatever it is that grown-ups say or do.

Still, when it came to physical contact, something was different here. My grandfather Pap and I are real close, but he never can really hug me because he has a hard time lifting his arms; he had polio when he was younger. Pap will put his arm on my shoulder and stuff like that, but he can't really hug me close or tight. I thought, Pap and I are really close, but he never puts his hand on my leg. So part of me thought it was strange that Jerry did that. But we were doing fun things and I continued to go with Jerry. I just decided not to pay attention to my own thoughts.

As that fall went on, Jerry started taking a few of us boys to his house, and then it was just me. The first time we were alone I think he took me swimming at the hotel and then to his house for dinner. His house was big, with a two-car garage, a real yard, and a basement that had a few rooms with a pool table, video games, and a water bed, and a small bathroom with a shower. It was the kind of basement rec area that I imagined rich kids had.

Jerry was really becoming like part of our family. He was calling Mom all the time to see how I was doing and how my brother and sister were doing. He even brought us an old computer and some books, and offered us tickets to Penn State games.

Jerry's wife, Dottie, was almost always at their house when I was there. Her name was Dottie, but everyone called her Sarge. I'm not sure why she had that nickname, and I never asked. Sarge was nice to me and a pretty good cook. I knew that Jerry and Sarge had kids they had adopted who were grown-up and living elsewhere. Sarge was okay. The only thing that I wondered about was why, even though it was her house, too, she never went down to the basement. It was like that was Jerry's place and not hers.

It's still hard for me to talk about it. I remember when it all started and how I was just so confused. At the time, "it" had no name. But now I know it was sexual abuse. It started for real in that basement. Whenever we were in the basement, we'd play darts and pool and shuffleboard and air hockey, and we'd be having a really good time. Then I'd go and take my shower before it was time for bed. I had my stuff with me because Jerry had gotten me started spending the night there. It was a treat for me, he said. He told my mom it wasn't a problem for him and his wife.

I'd take a shower in the basement bathroom, dry off with a towel, then put on my shorts and walk down the hallway into the big room, and then into the smaller basement room, where I slept on the water bed. Then Jerry would come down from upstairs. He'd crack my back, but then he started to lie on top of me on the bed. Sarge was always upstairs. When he lay on top of me, it didn't feel right, and I can't tell you why I still slept over, except that being at Jerry's and playing in that great basement room was fun. Jerry made it out like it was supposed to be special.

Jerry planned our weekends so that they became a routine, with things like playing catch or driving around. Like it was all just fine and good and right.

As the sleepover weekends went on, he started having me lie on top of him for a long period of time; he would just be lying there with his eyes closed as I did. I didn't know what to think about it. When I lay on top of him, I kept thinking that this feels too weird, and then I would talk myself out of thinking that way. My mind kept crisscrossing itself. I told myself that I just wasn't used to this kind of affection or something. It was like there were two voices. One was saying, "This is wrong and something bad is happening to you," and the other was saying, "No, it's fine. You're being stupid. Jerry is a really good guy."

I had that *uh-oh* feeling that I just kept squashing down, a feeling that the stuff he was doing was creepy and it wasn't just my imagination. But I let it go. I talked myself out of it. Even as I doubted him, I wondered why I felt so icky about what he was doing, as if maybe something was wrong with me instead of the other way around. When he reached down my pants and blew on my stomach and then kissed my lips, I just knew that something wasn't right, but by then a part of me was also scared of him.

Things got worse after that.

It really wasn't until I was fifteen and started seeing Mike that I realized the horror. Mike explained to me what Jerry's MO was and how it was the profile of a child predator. I felt angry. I also felt extremely stupid for not catching on sooner. For those times when Jerry started doing all those things to me that I knew deep down were just not right, and I spaced. I took myself out of my body and away from him and out of that basement room.

Let me put it this way for now. That first summer at camp I called Jerry Sandusky by his first name, like all of us kids did. Now I call him Monster.

3

Killers of the Soul

Mike

I'VE WORKED IN THIS FIELD FOR TWENTY-FIVE YEARS, AS A PSYCHO-logical associate since 1988 and a licensed psychologist since 1994. I've dealt with families in distress, domestic violence, and the physical and sexual abuse of children, and I have never seen a case as bad as Aaron's. This case was the absolute worst not only because the abuse went on for so long, but also because of the depth of the betrayal.

Right from the start, from the moment that Aaron started camp at the Second Mile, Jerry Sandusky set out with one purpose: the careful preparation of Aaron as his target. Sandusky had a plan that read like a blueprint for sexual abuse right from the start. He wanted Aaron to feel like Jerry was his best friend, his mentor, and that he was the only one who would ever be special in Aaron's life. He built things up gradually, knowing full well that Aaron was too young to know or question the normality of the sexual acts.

Sandusky's plan worked well in Aaron's case, as Aaron would later explain. He trusted Sandusky and assumed that everyone did those things in families. Although Aaron contended that he had Pap in his life, and that he never felt the absence of a father, since he never knew one in the first place, a fatherless boy is at a clear disadvantage when faced with the likes of a Jerry Sandusky.

Posing as the ultimate father figure, Sandusky guided Aaron into thinking this was all normal and natural. More than that, Aaron felt almost obligated because Sandusky was doing all these nice things for him—and who was Aaron to say no to anything that Sandusky wanted? I had seen this with other children. I see this sort of thing almost every day: someone older exploits a child and the child is unaware. But this was the first case I had ever seen of serial pedophilia.

The way in which Sandusky lured Aaron was a classic case of what is called child grooming. The pedophile subtly manipulates the child into trusting him and getting close to him emotionally. Sandusky created a strong bond with Aaron and then gradually desensitized him as he insidiously conditioned Aaron not only to comply with his sexual demands but also not to tell.

The process is such that the touching begins innocently, as though it could be perceived as an accident. In Aaron's case, it was an arm over the shoulder, tickling, a pat on the butt, a bear hug, and then it slowly escalated to a hand on a bare thigh, a kiss on the forehead, blowing on Aaron's stomach, and then a kiss on the lips.

The child is initially not as troubled as one might expect, because the pedophile's advancements to the next level are made slowly. In Aaron's case, Sandusky advanced to horrifying behavior—first to a lot of fondling and ultimately to oral sex, the latter of which began in the winter of 2006, when Aaron was twelve and Sandusky had his confused and easy prey sequestered in that basement room.

When Aaron explained and described Sandusky's phases and routines to me, I wasn't at all surprised. As Sandusky slowly intensified his repertoire, Aaron froze up. When I listened to Aaron, it was not unlike listening to a female talking about being raped. I have had many rape victims tell me that they left their body while the rape happened. The same thing happened with Aaron. He just took himself someplace else mentally. This response is a classic flight-or-fight reaction. Despite all the adrenaline flowing, victims find themselves unable to act. Freezing is also a form of flight.

But even before the touching began—again, as is the case generally with pedophiles—Sandusky ensured that Aaron was both endeared and obligated to him as he took him swimming and to ball games and hotels. Those feelings gave Sandusky time, since the more trust a victim feels the longer it takes him to feel certain that something is wrong. He left a vulnerable child in the position of feeling that what ultimately ensued sexually was normal, and although unknown territory to Aaron, it was something that Sandusky implied was to be expected. The duration of the abuse is beyond the scope of most pedophiles. Long-term abuse such as Aaron's is, however, in keeping with the profile of a serial pedophile, and we have now all come to know that Sandusky was one of the worst serial pedophiles in history.

I've explained this process of grooming to Aaron many times over his three years in therapy sessions. I have also explained how different a boy's frame of mind is at eleven or twelve, how it slowly changes at thirteen or fourteen, but that in the hands of a pedophile even a boy of slightly older age remains an unwitting captive. Younger boys as well as teenagers feel that something is "wrong" but neither group has developed sufficient self-esteem to rebel or fight back. And in Aaron's case, where the abuse started at such a young age, when he was a preteen and prepubescent, the self-esteem that might have been developing was eroded.

Kids are taught to respect adults who are in positions of authority. That the adult is right and the child has to respect them. As Aaron explained so often through tears, "Even though I felt weird, he was an adult and who was I to question what he was doing?"

Jerry Sandusky was not only an adult; he was also one of incredibly high standing. And what kid—or, as we found out later, what adult, even—would be bold enough to question him? Within the community, Sandusky was the guy with the heart of gold who founded the Second Mile. In Aaron's mind, he was the guy who was doing all these nice things for kids, the one who picked him as a favorite. Sandusky was spending his time and energy on Aaron, taking him to dinner, swimming, charity golf tournaments, college football games, and even NFL games, where he got to meet the Philadelphia Eagles. Who was Aaron to be so ungrateful as to question him? Terrifyingly, the very thought on the child's part that he should even consider questioning his abuser produces guilt. The child does not define the pedophile as an abuser.

There is also the sheer physical disparity between a boy and a man. Think about this: When Aaron was twelve and the abuse began in full, he weighed about seventy-five pounds and Sandusky weighed at least two hundred and fifty. Sandusky stood six foot two while Aaron was just shy of five feet.

Many children don't get past this. A great deal of the recovery depends on the child's support system, his parents, the individual, and therapy. Even those who follow through with therapy often resort to drugs and alcohol to escape. They just want to numb themselves and push away the unpleasant memories. Drugs and alcohol temporarily subdue the post-traumatic stress disorder. Many of the victims tell themselves that they're over it, but they're not. When the boys become men, they often attempt to secure their identities by having relationship after relationship with women, to the point of sexual addiction. Even from a single act of abuse, many individuals do not recover well.

The severe abuse and emotional injuries were inflicted upon Aaron during a critical period, the years from eleven to fifteen, and directly destroyed his development during that period. The post-traumatic stress that Aaron suffers will continue to rear its head throughout his life, as it does with other victims. He's made excellent strides, but healing is never really over.

The sexual abuse of a child is emotional homicide. Child abuse murders the soul.

4

The Taking of Innocence

Aaron

WHEN I CAME HOME FROM THOSE NIGHTS WITH JERRY, EVEN though I had a room to go to at home, I had a real hard time hanging out there. I needed to be outside and doing things. I needed to be in constant motion. I was always an athlete and loved wrestling and running track—really just about any kind of sports—but this feeling of needing movement was different.

I needed to get away from all the questions that I was asking myself. Sometimes I'd just go outside in the yard, but it was really best when I went to hang out with my friends and make things feel normal. I did whatever I could to get my mind off Jerry and all the guilt, shame, disgust, and embarrassment that kept welling up inside me after those weekends spent with him. I was good at pushing it all away. Or at least I thought I was good at it. Once the weekends were over, I managed to lock it all deep inside my mind somehow. That was how I dealt with it until the next time.

Mike has explained a lot of things to me since all this happened. He said that what I was doing is called compartmentalizing, and that physical exercise helps a lot, especially when it comes to anger. He said that a lot of kids do that with anger— even kids who weren't in my kind of situation. He said that was the reason that some kids throw snowballs at cars and then run and hide. It's a way of coping with stuff that's bothering you and making you frustrated and mad.

I remember one night when I went snowboarding with my friends through an old graveyard in town. We were weaving in and out on the hill where there were no tombstones so we wouldn't smash into anything, and it just felt so great. I felt safe that night, like my secret was tucked away; it felt good to know that in between the times with Jerry I could just act like it never happened and wouldn't happen again.

But it kept on happening. I was in such denial about everything. I didn't want to feel anything when it came to what was going on, and the more time went by, the more I knew that I couldn't get away from the fact that this was going on all the time and it shouldn't be.

I even started peeing in my bed when I was about twelve or so. Mom took me to the doctor, who said that was typical for a lot of boys my age and gave me a nasal spray he said would keep me from wetting. The doctor didn't ask me any questions about anything. If he had, I don't know if I could have answered them anyway.

I felt gross and just knew I couldn't tell anyone. And I don't think anyone could tell by looking at me. You couldn't tell by my actions until I was older when I couldn't take it anymore; that was when I really started acting out. I know now from Mike that Jerry had this routine. I know about all the textbook stuff that Mike has explained to me, but as the years with Jerry went by, I hurt so bad. Beyond Jerry scaring me with all the things he was doing to me, when I got older I didn't feel like myself anymore. I felt myself changing and that scared me as much as Jerry did. You have to understand that those years with Jerry blur together in my head.

Maybe it was because my mom and my teachers told me so or maybe it was because I felt that way myself, but in any case I was always considered to be that perfect child. I always did what I was told. I always listened to my mom and my teachers and my coaches. I was a good kid. There were other kids who smoked pot and used alcohol but I didn't. I didn't even smoke a cigarette, mostly because I was a runner. But all of a sudden as I got closer to fifteen, something changed in me.

I started being really disrespectful. I used bad language to my mom and sometimes just stormed out of the house for no reason at all, going wherever I wanted, whenever I wanted, no matter what my mom said to try to stop me.

Since I wasn't driving yet, I would just take off on foot and either walk the streets or go to a friend's house, or any other place that wasn't home. I even started acting out with Katie and Bubby; the three of us had this sort of deal that we could beat each other up, but if anybody outside of the three of us beat one of us up, that didn't fly. Not that I beat them up, but I wasn't nice to them. And that wasn't me. That's what I mean about those changes that I saw in myself. I was angry.

I was especially angry at my mom. I yelled at her when dinner wasn't on the table and told her that she didn't do anything all day long, so why didn't she have food there for me the minute I wanted it and how come she didn't have the foods that I liked? I criticized her when she was with her friends. Once the argument was done, and even if we both said we were sorry for fighting, I'd start up with something else and pick a new fight. I might tell her that I thought the house was a wreck and she was neglecting me and my siblings.

Mike explained that to me, too. He said that most teenagers get mad at their mothers for no reason at all. He said that's normal in adolescents anyway. Because he said that in some ways that behavior was typical, it felt good to know that back then at least a part of *me* was still typical, too. Jerry had taken most of the normal stuff away from me. Of course, Mike understood that I was also angry at Mom for different reasons. Mike and I have talked about that a lot and I get it.

On those nights and weekends when Jerry took me away, I wasn't computing it in my head as abuse. But deep down, I was angry at my mom because she wasn't stopping him. She didn't know what was going on but I wished that somehow she did.

Mom sent me to see a psychologist after months of my acting out. The psychologist told Mom that the reason I was acting out was that I was coming into puberty and also didn't have a man in the house. Mom's always been straight with me about everything, and she told me what that specialist said. I knew that was all wrong. The truth is, I felt like I was being neglected, and that no one was paying attention. No one would see what was happening.

I also came from a place where my mom and I used to do everything together. When she was sending me off with Jerry, I felt like she was having him do all the stuff with me instead of her. Then when I wanted her and needed her, I felt she wasn't around. I felt abandoned by her. It's like I was screaming that you have to see what is happening to me because look at how I'm acting and this isn't me and this isn't puberty and I don't need a father in my life so that's not it! I wanted to say how that behavioral therapist got it all wrong. But I couldn't.

So no one saw, or maybe no one wanted to see because it was the kind of stuff that would have been hard to believe, especially with a guy like Jerry Sandusky. One time when Jerry and I were in that basement room and he was the middle of what he did to me, a table broke upstairs. Sarge called down to the basement for Jerry and asked if he would come up and fix it. Jerry said he was fixing the air hockey table and couldn't help her right then. She just let it go. In my memory, she never called to him again when he was in the basement with me.

Sarge never went down to the basement. No matter what. Maybe she went down there when no one was home, but she sure didn't go when other kids and I were there. At first I tried to figure out why, and then as I got older and was trying to stay away from him, I thought, What if his whole family was in on what was happening to me? What if they all just know that he brings kids like me here and they let him get away with what he does to kids like me? I wondered if that was how it worked in Jerry's family—a kind of conspiracy. So many things were running through my head and I didn't want to believe half of what I thought, but then I started to believe that Sarge wasn't coming down to the basement for the very reason that she knew. Somewhere deep inside me, I thought she had to know.

The lawyers asked me at the trial and at the grand juries how many times Jerry had molested me. They asked me how many times oral sex happened between us, and when I couldn't answer that question because it just made me sick, they asked me in terms of numbers: Was it more than ten times? Was it upwards of twenty-four times? Finally I said yes to upwards of twenty-four times; they accepted that answer and didn't ask anymore. I guess that general number of times was good enough. Well, it was actually hundreds of times, but that's upwards of twenty-four, right?

When it started getting clearer that something really bad was going on, I was afraid that no one would ever believe me if I had the nerve to say what he was doing to me. He wasn't just any man. This was Jerry Sandusky, the man who had done all this great stuff for Penn State football and started the camp for kids like me. He'd even written a book. He was famous and everyone looked up to him like he was God. I knew that. So who would possibly believe me? I knew even then that I would be one small person going up against him. But when I was about to turn fifteen, I was old enough to know how sick it all was, and it made me want to throw up. I wanted to stay away from him. This was after three years of abuse. It took that long, but there's a big difference between twelve and almost fifteen. At some point I snapped; it was like my mind said, "Look, you get out or we're shutting you down."

Sure, he took me places and introduced me to athletes like the Philadelphia Eagles and we went on a trip for some charity golf tournament in Maryland, but I didn't care anymore about what he'd done for me. Suddenly I cared about what he was doing to me. I had to get out but I wasn't sure how.

I also wasn't sure how was I going to explain to my mom the reason I didn't want to go with Jerry anymore. I was afraid to tell her.

When I first told Jerry that I didn't want to do this anymore, we were in that basement room and he got rough with me. He got in my face and started screaming at me and grabbed my arms so hard that he left bruises on me. It was the first time I rejected him and he was mad. At first, I had just gone and hid in one of the other little rooms in the basement, and he thought we were playing some sort of game. When he realized that I wasn't playing and that I meant it, he grabbed me and said something like I needed to behave since he does all kinds of nice things for me; I was being ungrateful and needed to cooperate with him.

I finally told my mom that I was getting tired of being with Jerry and that I just wanted to hang out with my friends. I said to tell Jerry that I wasn't home even if I was when he called.

It was around the end of the summer. I was fourteen, and would be fifteen in November. At that point, I even signed up for this program at Big Brother/Big Sisters where I could hang out and play pool and games and do my homework after school. We went bowling and to movies and roller-skating; it was good but it was most of all a good excuse not to be with Jerry.

The next time Jerry called, Mom said I was out, even though I was home. He demanded to know where I was and she told him that I was getting older and just wanted to hang out with my friends. That was when Jerry went crazy.

5

It Doesn't Matter
Who He Is

Dawn

THE NOTION THAT JERRY WOULD HARM MY CHILD NEVER CROSSED my mind. Maybe if he hadn't been Jerry Sandusky I would have felt different. I'm still not sure. I think I still would have trusted him even if he was just the guy who ran a children's camp, and nothing more. This was a man who had a special interest in kids—so, in my mind, why would he hurt them?

And in the beginning, he was a gentleman. He didn't overstep his bounds with me or with my kids. He even signed up Katie and Bubby for the "friend" program at the Second Mile. So it wasn't like he was just taking an interest in Aaron; he was taking an interest in the welfare of my other kids, not to mention everyone else's kids.

The first time that Aaron spent the night at Jerry's house, I knew that there were other kids there. I also knew that he was a married man and that he and his wife had raised six adopted children. His wife's name was Dottie but everyone called her Sarge. I always wondered why, and much later I found out that it was because she had a reputation for being strict. I met Sarge briefly that first night when I dropped Aaron off, so I also knew that she would be there. Having a "mother" at home made a difference to me.

One time, when Jerry took Aaron and some other kids to swim and for dinner, Jerry called me to say that for some reason the pool was closed, so was it all right if he took them all to his house instead to play video games? Of course I didn't mind. How generous of him was that? And how polite he was to ask my permission first. Another time, I had to go over to Jerry's to pick something up that Aaron had left behind. As I recall, Aaron had not yet spent the night there, and while Jerry went to get whatever Aaron left, I sat in the living room and talked to Sarge. I was playing with their Saint Bernard and trying to make conversation, and I thought that Sarge was kind of mean. She just rubbed me the wrong way. That first time I saw her was just a brief hello, but this was the first time we ever really talked. Even though she was polite, she wasn't warm. Jerry, on the other hand, was extremely warm. They were very different.

After Aaron started to spend a lot of time at their house and began staying the night, whenever I saw Sarge, I always felt like she was treating me as though I was the "other woman." It almost reminded me of the way my husband's ex-wife used to treat me. I felt self-conscious. I thought maybe she was jealous of me. I asked Aaron if she was mean to him and he said that she wasn't, and that he really liked her cooking.

I had a funny feeling from Sarge because she was just so cold. It crossed my mind that maybe Sarge was nasty to me because she was a snob, that she looked down her nose at me because I wasn't on her level. I thought maybe she was jealous because her husband spent so much time with my kid and Jerry was over at our house a lot, too. I just couldn't figure her out.

Looking back, I think that maybe Sarge treated me bad because part of her knew what was going on.

Even so, Jerry gave me hope and I trusted him. One time Jerry and Sarge even babysat my other kids. I was working the beer cart at a fund-raiser for my daughter's cheerleading team and I dropped off Katie and Bubby at the Sanduskys' since the two kids weren't old enough to be home on their own. Jerry had offered to keep an eye on them and then bring them over to me when the fund-raiser was finished. He said there was no reason for me to drive back and forth.

When Aaron first started spending so many nights at Jerry's, I asked Jerry if that was okay and not an imposition. Jerry was again reassuring. He said they had a spare bedroom in the basement with a water bed, video games, and everything and that Aaron was happy and safe and clean, so I shouldn't worry.

When Aaron came home from those nights at Jerry's, I didn't notice anything different about him. Now, I have other kids and they've spent the night at their friends' houses or at their grandparents, and with Aaron it would be kind of like when any of my kids came back from any sleepovers. You let your kid go someplace where there are different rules; when they come home and back to your rules, they're ornery, because it was more fun at someone else's house. When Aaron was with my parents, they spoiled him; he got everything he wanted when he was there, and when he came home to me, it was the same old, same old. I figured that was the case when he was at Jerry's, too, so I didn't pay attention if he was kind of cranky. I thought he liked it better at Jerry's, where he was the center of attention and not one of three kids. He'd act out a little but I figured it was just that transition between being at Jerry's and being at home.

Aaron started wetting the bed at twelve. That was just around the time he started staying over at Jerry's, but at the time I never made the connection. He never told me when he wet the bed, because he was embarrassed, but I would find his sheets wet so I knew. I took him to our pediatrician, Dr. Turner. The doctor said it wasn't uncommon at all. Aaron had wet the bed when he was younger, but then he had stopped, so I was worried that there was something physically wrong with him. However, Dr. Turner explained that sometimes bladders grow at a slow rate and can't hold the pee; he gave Aaron a nose spray and said that should help. All I could think was that when he was at Jerry's he was probably wetting the bed, too, so I made sure he took the nose spray with him when he slept there. I asked Aaron if he wet the bed at Jerry's; Aaron said that he did sometimes, but Jerry and Sarge never said anything to him about it.

I told Jerry about taking Aaron to the doctor for the bedwetting and he asked me what the doctor said. Jerry said that boys do that sometimes and I shouldn't worry about it. He even said that he knew Aaron wet and tried to hide it, but that it wasn't a problem for him. He was used to it with boys Aaron's age. Jerry was comforting and had all the right answers.

One afternoon, Jerry was over at our apartment, and when he heard that Katie was on the cheerleading team, he asked her to teach him some of her jumps. Then he started doing cheers for all of my kids. He was jumping around and making up a cheer like "Jerry! Jerry! He's our man! He can do what no one can!" I thought that was really bizarre. I even told my friends about it afterward and said that I wondered if Jerry was gay. I still didn't find him threatening in any way, but I wondered if he was someone other than what he presented himself to be.

One of my neighbors, when I told him about Jerry doing the cheers, said, "Wouldn't it be something if he was molesting kids?"

I felt myself clutch and then I asked him why he would say something like that. He said, "Nah, I'm just joking and being a jerk."

But after he said it, I called my best friend Kathy and told her what the neighbor said and then we both said, "Oh no, that's crazy. I mean really crazy. I mean, this is Jerry Sandusky we're talking about."

Still, it bothered me enough that I even asked Aaron if he thought that Jerry liked guys or if he did any stuff that's sexual to him. Aaron said no and told me I was crazy.

I've since learned the difference between being gay and being a pedophile.

I never thought that Jerry was the brightest person in the world. He didn't speak the way someone in his position should speak and instead acted like a big kid. He didn't seem sophisticated. I just took him to be a real dumb jock with a heart of gold.

As time went on and Aaron was around thirteen or so, he really started to act out and give me a hard time. He was mouthing off to me and even called me a bitch once and screamed at me. Once he even hit me. This was totally new behavior and I figured I should call the school. I called the psychologist at the middle school and asked him to evaluate Aaron. He met with him and afterward said it was just puberty; boys go through that, and especially because there's no father in the house, it might be worse and I should just let it go.

The school knew that Aaron spent a lot of time with Jerry and that Jerry was mentoring him, because Jerry often picked him up from school and he was very visible in Aaron's life. He even watched him at practices and drove him home. I didn't know that Jerry was driving Aaron home in those days until all of this came out. I never gave Jerry permission to drive him home. Often, when I went to the middle school because Aaron had left something at home, like his wrestling shoes, and I had to drop them off, Jerry was there. He'd ask me if I was there because Aaron got in trouble. I explained that Aaron forgot something. I never asked Jerry why *he* was there. I knew that he volunteer-coached at the school and figured that was reason enough.

During this time, when Aaron was with Jerry, I was dealing with my daughter. I had to keep track of her mobile therapist and her behavioral specialist and her post-traumatic stress disorder workers, who were in my house working with her all the time. Katie's PTSD started after Eric physically abused her and I threw him out. I would only allow supervised visits with him. But Katie still didn't want to be around him and used to hold on to the car and I would have to peel her off and make her go and she would scream. I took the mobile therapist into court with me and she explained that Katie was now afraid of men and then the judge said that Katie did not have to go on the visits even when they're supervised. The judge said Katie could get gifts or cards or phone calls from Eric but that was it. So I had my hands full with my daughter. I was distracted for sure.

There came a time when Aaron stopped wanting or agreeing to be with Jerry. I didn't keep a journal back then, but I know that Aaron was closer to fifteen. He didn't say straight out that he didn't want to go with Jerry, but he would just say, "If Jerry calls, tell him I'm busy." He was still wetting the bed and he had been hanging out with Jerry for about three years now, and suddenly he tells me that he needs me to lie to Jerry for him. I asked why did I have to lie to him and why don't you just tell him that you don't want to go? Aaron says it's because you can't tell Jerry stuff like that. I brought it up to Aaron again and again asked why he didn't want to go with Jerry anymore and he said because Jerry wanted Aaron to be with him every weekend and he just didn't want to be there every weekend—he wanted to be with his friends. That made sense to me. He was getting older. Aaron also didn't want to go to the Second Mile anymore. He'd been there for three summers at that point and he wanted to go to wrestling camp. He also wanted to go to the after-school program at Big Brothers/Big Sisters.

I assumed Aaron didn't want to tell Jerry himself because he didn't want to hurt his feelings, since this guy was spending all this time with him and doing stuff with him and he didn't want to be disrespectful.

So, I lied to Jerry for Aaron. When Jerry called, I would tell him that Aaron wasn't home even when he was and then Jerry would ask me for his friend's phone number so he could call him at his friend's house. I thought that was awkward. Why would he hunt him down at a friend's house? I said to Jerry, why don't you just call somebody else? I told Jerry that I didn't want to disrespect him but Aaron was hanging out with his friends and then I'd end the conversation.

But the more that Aaron didn't want to be with Jerry, the more Jerry called. Sometimes he called several times a day. He was real upset and when I got defensive and even bitchy and asked him what was the big deal if Aaron didn't want to go with him, he said that he had a tight schedule and really needed Aaron's help because Aaron promised to help him with certain things at the camp and at golf tournaments. He said that he paid Aaron to manage equipment and such but I never knew about that arrangement. He made it out like Aaron had made a commitment to help him and was skipping out on it and being irresponsible. He made it sound like he was doing this for Aaron's own good. Like even though he was a kid, he had an obligation to do what he promised.

Aaron started acting out even more with me and when I grounded him for that, Jerry got real upset. He wanted me to lift that grounding because he wanted to be with him, but I said Aaron's grades are bad and he's mouthing off and I'm his mother and he's not going anywhere. Jerry said how about if I make sure he gets his grades up and talk to him about the way he's been treating you? Then will you let him come with me? I said that I would, but I'd also have to speak to Aaron's teachers. Then, if Aaron met all the conditions, he could go with Jerry.

Until then, Aaron never told me that he didn't want to see Jerry *at all* anymore. He just said he didn't want to be with him so much and wanted to be with his friends more. A teenager wanting to be with his friends more than with an adult didn't seem strange to me.

I told Aaron what Jerry's deal was when it came to his being grounded and that was when Aaron dug in his heels. He said that I needed to tell Jerry that he wasn't home because he wasn't going with him despite the paying job. He just didn't want to be with Jerry and he made that clear to me. So, even though I told

Jerry that he could see Aaron if he had a talk with him, when he called the house, I continued to say that Aaron wasn't there.

It wasn't much later on that Jerry followed Aaron's school bus home and came to my house looking for Aaron. He stood in my front yard and demanded to know where Aaron was. Aaron had just walked home from the bus stop and I saw him dart behind a bush when he saw Jerry. I sort of jerked my head to say "run in the house." I still wasn't thinking too much of anything other than that Aaron didn't want to be with him and I was protecting my child's wishes.

I was talking to Jerry outside and he was nearly begging me, saying that he just wanted to talk to Aaron, and I kept saying he's not home. I said I didn't know where he was and Jerry got real agitated but he tried to calm himself down. He said that he wasn't trying to get at him and maybe Aaron was mad at him because he was coming on a little too strong about all the responsibility stuff. He even admitted that Aaron ran from him at school and that he was just trying to schedule stuff with him and couldn't get a straight answer out of him. I laughed and said that Aaron was a teenager and I couldn't get straight answers from him either.

That might have been the first moment when I thought that I've got to keep my kid away from this guy, but I didn't know exactly what my instinct was telling me. I was just talking to him and explaining that Aaron was a teenager now and his life was changing and Jerry wasn't getting it. I was intimidated by Jerry but I was also confused and wondering why he was acting that way.

Jerry apologized and walked off and said he was going to go and look for Aaron. I went back in the apartment and told Aaron that he had to come right out and tell Jerry that he didn't want to see him and he should also find out what he wanted. At that point, Jerry had come back and that was when Aaron went outside to talk to him.

I was peeking at them through the window. I could see Jerry's hand motions and he was yelling, and even though I couldn't hear his exact words, I could tell that he was angry. So then I went upstairs and opened my bedroom window and stood and listened and I heard him telling Aaron that he was being ridiculous and that he needed to spend more time with him and that Aaron's joining other programs makes him feel useless.

That was when I called my dad. Jerry was trying to act like a parent and I thought Aaron's my child and no one else is going to make demands on my child but me. I resented him for the way he was acting with my kid and yet I didn't feel right standing up to him because of who he was.

My dad came right over because he could hear that I was scared and Dad knows that I don't scare easy. I wanted to go outside and just tell Jerry to get away from my kid but I couldn't because he was Jerry Sandusky.

Aaron went back into the house before my dad got there and I went back outside to talk to Jerry while I waited for Dad. I saw Aaron watching from the window, and Jerry was pacing in a circle like a caged animal while I tried to calm him down. He was wearing his usual outfit of a white T-shirt and blue wind pants and he was just so frantic. He reminded me of someone who was being accused in a domestic dispute.

When my dad pulled up, I said you've got to get out of the car and talk to Jerry and even though that's hard for Dad because he has polio, he climbed out of the car. Dad asked him what the problem was and then Jerry gave this sort of jock giggle and said it wasn't such a big deal that my dad needed to come over, and then he went into the whole routine about being a busy guy and how he just needed Aaron to make a schedule with him because he's trying to give him as much time as possible. He said that even going to wrestling camp for a week wasn't a real good idea because it would cut into their schedule. Jerry acted like he was trying to rescue Aaron and I was trying to stop him. He acted like he was our salvation. I went back inside after that. I'd heard enough.

My dad and Jerry must have been there for well over an hour when I came back out. I was beginning to get pissed off and frustrated. I didn't want to challenge Jerry too much but I did tell him that I wasn't trying to be ignorant, that I am Aaron's mom and it's my job to handle things. He said he wasn't trying to step on my toes, he was just trying to help. My dad said that all Jerry was trying to do was schedule time with Aaron. How Jerry said he could take other kids but he sees something in Aaron and wants to make sure that he stays on the right path and he just wants to help and he really cares about him.

Looking back, I think Jerry was scared that day. I think he was afraid that he was going to be caught. I mean, he came to my house and apologized for chasing Aaron that day and admitted that he followed Aaron's school bus home. He apologized in front of me and my father. He kept saying that he wasn't trying to make anyone mad and insisting that he was just trying to help.

After Jerry and I argued that whole time, I finally just said, You know what? I'm done. He's almost fifteen and he wants to be with his friends. None of his friends are hanging out with a sixty-year-old guy. They're with their friends and doing bike jumps. And Aaron is obligated to go to wrestling camp. My dad was quiet and he listened and then he said again how I also have to understand that Jerry is a busy man and it would help him if Aaron would schedule with him. I said that was fine but he'll schedule when he's ready because there are other things he wants to do. I said that my dad was a candyland grandfather and Jerry wanted to be one too, and that no one decides what's best for Aaron except for me and that he doesn't need another candyland grandfather type in his life.

Jerry asked to talk to Aaron again, but I said he couldn't because everyone needs to cool down and that Aaron will call when he's ready. Jerry accepted that and then he left. Dad left after

Jerry, but before he did I asked what he thought. He said it was all kind of strange, but he thought that Jerry was just a busy guy with good intentions.

From that day forward, I had real suspicions about Jerry. I didn't exactly know what they were, but I know now that they were all wrong.

Aaron was still avoiding Jerry after that day and still not wanting to go with him. He saw him one time after that in my memory. It was a Sunday morning and Jerry took Aaron to church. As far as I knew, Aaron didn't go to church, and when I asked him why he was going, he said because that's what Jerry does. He said they'd gone to church before on Sundays.

It wasn't long after that when Aaron finally broke down.

6

Crying for Help

Aaron

JERRY WENT SO CRAZY WHEN I TRIED TO AVOID HIM THAT HE started coming to the school and telling the principal that he needed to talk to me about something or other. The principal would call me out of class even though school rules said you could only skip out if it was an emergency or during study period or lunch. But because Jerry was who he was, the teachers always let me go. Everyone bent the rules when it came to Jerry Sandusky.

Sometimes when they called me down for Jerry, I went and hid in the bathroom. And no one asked me why. The worst part was that all the kids in school thought I was a problem kid. Why else was I called to the principal's office? And my grades were slipping, too. No one asked me why that was happening, either.

I'd get down to the office and Jerry would want to know why I wasn't scheduling time with him. I knew that by coming to my school like that Jerry was stalking me, but I couldn't say anything. I knew that if I said anything to the principal, I'd be asked a million questions, and I wasn't ready to say anything about what he did to me. I was trying to avoid Jerry as best I could but he wasn't giving up.

One day I was taking the bus home and I noticed that a car pulled out into the bus lanes at the school as the buses were getting ready to leave. I saw that the security guard let the car through even though cars weren't allowed in those lanes. Our bus had two other buses behind it, then this car, which I could have sworn was Jerry's. I told myself that I was being paranoid; it's just a car that looks like his and sometimes cars get in the bus lanes by accident.

When the other buses pulled onto the highway for their usual routes, it was just our bus at the intersection with that familiar car again. I was talking to my friends on the bus and we were all fooling around, but now I was certain it was Jerry's car.

I had planned to get off at my buddy's stop that day because he hadn't been in school and I wanted to see what was going on. I thought maybe he was sick, and I just wanted to see if he was home. Even if he was sick, we could hang out. Anything was better than going home. When I got to my friend's, no one was there, so I figured I'd just head home. As I was walking down the main street that leads straight to my house, Jerry's car came around the corner, whipped into a side street where I had to cross, and stopped. Yes, it was that same car I saw in the bus lanes. See, Jerry Sandusky can go anywhere—even in bus lanes where no cars are allowed.

I knew that Jerry had me cornered and wanted to talk to me. I didn't want to talk to him. I had nothing to say to him. He rolled down the passenger window and commanded me to stop. He was all red in the face, like he was going to burst. So I stopped and talked to him. He said that he didn't like that I was avoiding him. I said that I was just busy with my friends; I wanted to hang out with them and do the stuff that kids do. It seemed like he didn't hear a word I was saying. He said that I still needed to schedule time with him. I told him I was going home. At that point he screamed at me to get in the car, but I just turned and started walking away.

Jerry's car made this whirring noise when it was in reverse gear. As I walked away, I heard his car start backing up and I knew he was trying to catch me. By the time he got close to me, I just took off running. I was on the track team at this point, a standout distance runner, so I could run fast. I cut through a little alley where cars can't go; he cut through another street on the other side of the alley. I hoped I'd get home before he cornered me again. I guess my detour was a longer way home. When I got there, I saw Jerry's car. He was standing in front of my house talking to my mom, so I hid behind a bush. My mom saw me hiding but didn't let on to Jerry, who was obviously upset. Mom kind of jerked her head real slightly to the side and motioned to me to run around the back of the house. I sneaked back there fast while she kept Jerry distracted.

Once I was inside, I started listening to their conversation from the window. My mom said she didn't understand why Jerry was acting that way; I could see that she was pretty confused. Jerry told her he needed me to schedule time with him. He also said that he was paying me for some odd jobs and I was being irresponsible about doing them. At that point I came outside and said how I am a kid and I do things with my friends and there are other things I want to do instead of being with him. By that point Mom had gone back into the house. Later I learned it was to call Pap.

Jerry just kept screaming at me. I said I was sorry but I wanted to do what kids do. I don't know what finally gave me the courage to confront him. I've never liked being yelled at, but until then I was afraid of Jerry.

Pap came over and asked Jerry what this was all about. Jerry toned it down and made it sound like he was just trying to schedule time with me because he was a busy man and I was a kid and I needed to go by his schedule. Because I was yelling at Jerry in front of Pap, Pap sort of agreed with Jerry that I shouldn't get so worked up.

Later, Pap told Mom and me that it was really just a big fuss over nothing. He's old-school, I guess. Jerry was, after all, Jerry, and Pap figured I was just being a kid.

After that day, I never went to Jerry's house again and I tried to avoid him altogether. There was one Sunday when I agreed to go with him to church. Jerry went to church regularly every Sunday. The only reason I agreed to go was because after his outburst in our yard, I was still afraid that Jerry might hurt me or my family. Going with him to church that last time was like my saying, *Okay. I'll do this with you, but this is the last thing I will ever do with you.* Another time, he had me pulled out of class to talk to me. And then one last time, even though I was about to get on the bus, he drove me home because I couldn't turn down the ride with everyone watching. I didn't want to make a scene in front of the other kids.

He sent me gifts after that, like a set of golf clubs and a card with about forty dollars in it. Now that I think about it, he was like a clingy girlfriend asking, Why won't you see me anymore? But I was too young to pick up on that at the time.

I could see how desperate he was, and it scared me to death. I knew he was out of control.

But I think my mom was more curious than she was suspicious, until about a month after that afternoon when Jerry was at our house with Pap and Mom.

I had recently taken a class in which they told us about websites where you can look up sex offenders. I'd also heard about those websites on TV, and I knew that Mom checked them out, because one time she looked up this creepy guy who was hanging around the playground, and sure enough, she found his picture on one of those websites and called the police.

It was November and I was just about to turn fifteen. And suddenly something clicked in my head. When I went home that day, Mom and her friend Kathy were sitting and talking in the living room. The computer was on a small table in the corner by the kitchen door, but really in the same room as Mom and Kathy. As I sat down in front of it, I asked Mom what the website was where she read about people who did bad things to kids. I said, "You know, like people who are sexual weirdos." She asked if I meant the website for Megan's Law, and I said yeah, I want to look up someone on there. Mom started to laugh and asked me who I wanted to look up. I said I wanted to see if Jerry was on there. She said, "You want to look up Jerry Sandusky on a sex offender's site?" She laughed again.

I said that I just wondered whether he was on there. Mom told me that he wouldn't be on that site unless he had been convicted, and Jerry wouldn't be at the Second Mile if he was a convicted sex offender because a sex offender couldn't be around kids. She asked me if I was saying that he's a sex offender and I said I wasn't saying that. I was just saying that he's weird, that's all. Then I got mad and shoved the keyboard and went outside to hang out with my friends.

I was angry. To tell you the truth, I felt my mom wasn't doing her part to protect and help me. How could she still let me keep going off with him? Why wasn't she there to stop him? I said it to her in words once, after the fact. I told her exactly that one day when we were arguing. I said it was her fault that all this happened because she allowed me to go with him even when I didn't want to go and she should have known or picked up on it somehow. We were always close, my mom and me, but during those three years, as Jerry's abuse intensified, I went through a very bad phase with her.

But that day after I wanted to look up what I called the sex weirdos, I was angrier than I'd ever been. How could no one see what was happening? All that rage that was pent up in me for years when I yelled at Mom for not having the right food in the house or not acting the way I wanted her to. When she would sit and talk to a friend or hang out with neighbors, like nothing at all was wrong. And now I was asking to look up sex offender websites and still nothing?

After my little brother and sister went to sleep that night, Mom came into my room. I told her that I was just upset because Jerry was coming to the school and pulling me out of classes so he could talk to me about stuff and that the principal was allowing it because he was Jerry Sandusky. I said how the other kids thought I was in trouble because any kid who goes to the principal's office must be there because he's a bad kid.

I didn't have the guts to tell her what was really going on. At that point, she did ask me if Jerry had done anything to me that was sexual and I just said no. I couldn't look her in the eye, and maybe that could have been a clue, but I stuck to my story about being pegged as a bad kid and not liking that.

Mom said that she'd call the school in the morning and make sure that Jerry wouldn't take me out of classes anymore. She said that she'd fix the problem. But I knew that she couldn't possibly fix what was really happening to me. I didn't think that anyone could.

7

Too Little, Too Late

Dawn

So, there I was with Kathy after Aaron wanted to search the site for Megan's Law. As soon as he left the apartment and slammed the door shut, I turned to her and said, "No way. Why would he ask that?" I had laughed when he told me. At first I thought he asked because he was in the park playing football and chase that day and there was this guy who hung out in the park who was on the website. He used to go to that park and I called the police on him once when we lived down there, because if you're a registered sex offender you can't be hanging out with kids or around kids. I assumed that was why he wanted to look at the website. I figured that creepy guy was there. But Jerry? On the Megan's Law site?

I sat there with Kathy and started thinking back; things were flashing in my mind. I was thinking, Oh my God. I started thinking about the relationship between Aaron and Jerry, and as I talked to Kathy, she said, "You're really going to have to grill Aaron when he gets home." I wondered how I could possibly ask him anything like that.

That night, I waited until the other kids were in bed and then I went to Aaron's room. I said that people don't just ask stuff like that, about looking up someone on a sex offender website, for no reason. I told him that if something did happen to him, he needed to tell me. Aaron said it wasn't like that, and that Jerry was just weird. I said if something is going on, I can't help you unless you tell me. He said, "You can't help me anyway," and then he started to cry. He said that Jerry was taking him out of classes and teachers hated him now at school and the kids hated him because he wasn't in class a lot because of Jerry. It almost didn't make sense. But he said that was the reason he didn't want to hang out with Jerry anymore. I said, "So that's it? That's the reason?" He said yes and then I asked him why the school allowed Jerry to pull him out of class. He said usually it was Assistant Principal Turchetta who called him out whenever Jerry wanted to see him because Jerry is Jerry. But all the kids thought it was because Aaron was trouble and a bad kid; why else would the principal want to see him?

I told him that he wasn't a bad kid and he should know that. He repeated again that the teachers and kids were giving him attitude, thinking maybe he was some kind of troublemaker. Then he got more worked up and said that because Jerry was constantly pulling him from class, he had missed lessons and that's why his grades were slipping. And then I asked him why Jerry was pulling him from class. Aaron said that Jerry gave him money and wanted to schedule stuff with him but he didn't want to schedule with Jerry anymore. We just kept going round and round.

I told Aaron that there was no way that Jerry was getting a free pass from the principal and that I would call the school first thing in the morning and fix this. I said I am your mother and under no circumstances will Jerry be allowed to take you out of class anymore.

Aaron just looked up at me and asked if I could really do that, and I told him that I could. Then I asked him, for sure, if that was what all this was about, and he said yes, and please let's not talk about it anymore; he was beginning to get irritated. I dropped it.

I still didn't know what was going on, but at that point I had a sense that there was more to what Aaron had told me. I was up all night that night, going over everything in my mind. At that point, I was trying to shake off the notion that maybe Aaron had been molested. I still wasn't sure if it was sexual or physical abuse but I had never noticed any physical evidence of anything on Aaron. I never saw any bruises or cuts. I was going nuts thinking about why he wanted to look up "sex weirdos." Then I went through the call logs on my cellphone and thought how crazy this was until I saw that Jerry had called eighteen times in the week before. Everything seemed to be adding up in my head, but Aaron still hadn't told me anything and this was a kid who I thought had always told me everything. I never figured that in a million years . . . But my mind kept coming back to a single, unbearable thought. Why wouldn't he say something to me?

I called the school first thing in the morning and spoke to the principal, Karen Probst, who said I really needed to talk to Mrs. Smith, the guidance counselor, as well. They put me on a speakerphone conference call so I could talk to them both at once, and I basically told them that Aaron expressed to me that Jerry Sandusky was taking him out of class, that Aaron didn't like missing classes, and that the other kids were thinking he was always in trouble.

I said that something just didn't feel right, and then I told them how Jerry had come to our house and argued with me and with Aaron because Aaron didn't want to spend as much time with Jerry anymore now that he was getting older. He wanted to be with his friends.

Finally, I said, look, I am going to lay it right out how I feel. I didn't say that Jerry Sandusky was molesting my son but I did say that as a mother I was seeing some signs that I questioned. Here's Jerry Sandusky coming to my house and arguing with me about seeing my son, and pulling him out of class, and here's my son acting out—and then he comes home yesterday and wants to look up sex offenders?

Karen Probst said, well, maybe Jerry Sandusky comes on a little too strong, but that man has a heart of gold and he would never do anything to any child.

Heart of gold. That's what everyone always said.

I said that I wasn't making any accusations but I just had a bad feeling, and Jerry shouldn't be allowed to take Aaron out of class anymore. Karen said that it was not uncommon for Jerry to do that with some kids. I said, well, not with my kid. I insisted that Aaron was not to be taken out of classes unless it was at my request.

I felt like I was getting resistance from both Karen and Mrs. Smith. Finally, they admitted that because Aaron's grades were slipping as a result of missing class, they'd make sure that Jerry didn't pull him out again. I asked them to call Aaron into the office during lunch period so that Mrs. Smith could talk to him and find out what was going on, because I just had a gut feeling that there was something Aaron wasn't telling me. I said to just ask him how he feels about Jerry.

Karen Probst called me a couple of hours later. She sounded like she was in tears. For sure, she was very upset. She said that I needed to come to the school right away. I started to cry and asked if Aaron was okay. All she said again was that I needed to get to the school *right away.*

During that ten-minute drive to the school I felt sick, like I was going to have to pull over and throw up. At that point, I knew—one hundred percent—that something had happened. Whatever doubts I ever had were gone.

I pulled into the parking lot and went to the main office, where someone was waiting to escort me to Mrs. Smith's office. Aaron was sitting there with his backpack at his feet and he was in tears, just staring down at the floor. Mrs. Smith and Karen looked like they had been crying or were trying real hard not to in front of Aaron. They both hugged me. I said, "He did something to him, didn't he?"

Karen said that Aaron had something he needed to tell me. She said he had told them some things, but he had to tell me, too.

Aaron started to cry and then he said, "I had to stop it. I just had to stop it."

I asked him, "Stop what?"

"I had to stop it because it was only going to get worse," he said, sobbing.

I asked him if Jerry was doing sexual stuff to him and he said yes.

I turned to Karen and asked her what we were going to do now. Were we going to call the police? And Karen said we needed to go home and get collected. She said that everyone is very emotional right now and we need you to go home and think about all this, about what we want to do and how we want to handle this.

I said no, we should call the police right now. She said that we couldn't do that right now. I got louder and started screaming, "We are calling the fucking police right now!" And Aaron was crying again and saying that they didn't believe him.

I told Karen and Mrs. Smith that there was nothing to think about, that this man did something to my child. They actually said that this man is Jerry Sandusky and he spends a lot of time with a lot of kids and you need to think about the repercussions.

Now, understand that both Karen and Mrs. Smith are on the verge of tears. *And still they're talking to me about repercussions.* Repercussions, I suppose, because the notion that Jerry Sandusky could be a child molester was unthinkable. I was so very confused by them, but I said I don't care who he is; we need to call the police. Karen still said no. She said to take Aaron and go home and we'll decide what to do tomorrow, when everyone is calmer. Then we'll call you and discuss this.

I was so mad I was swearing. I told Aaron to get his stuff and we left. On our way out, I called Erin Rutt from my cell. Erin and I had become friendly because she worked as a staff coordinator at Big Brothers/Big Sisters and really ran the program. She also worked as a volunteer for the Second Mile. I felt that Erin was in a position to know something and do something—more than my dad or Kathy was. I had told Erin how Jerry acted upset when I wanted to sign Aaron up for Big Brothers/Big Sisters, and she couldn't understand why he wouldn't want Aaron in that program, since it was so good. Later that day, after we found out what was going on for sure, Erin told me how she had thought Jerry acted peculiar the day she was at my house doing Big Brothers/Big Sisters intakes for Katie and Bubby. Jerry was there, and even though he knew Erin pretty well from the Second Mile, he acted like they were strangers. That was another missed red flag.

As I drove Aaron home from school he sat in the front seat with his hands over his face. He was crying and saying over and over again that he knew they wouldn't believe him. Erin met us at the house and then drove us to Children and Youth Services in Lock Haven. Children and Youth is a county-wide organization and provides protection. I swear I couldn't breathe. I definitely couldn't drive.

When we got to Children and Youth, an intake worker tried to talk to Aaron, but he wouldn't open up at all. They called the psychologist, who turned out to be Mike Gillum, who then took Aaron into his office upstairs. He said they needed to talk alone. I wanted to be in there with him but Mike said it was better if they were one-on-one; he'd talk to me afterward. Erin tried to calm me down and we took seats in a waiting area. But I couldn't sit still. I was irate. I was scared and I knew that Aaron was scared and I wasn't feeling real confident about Mike. At that point, I had no faith in anything or anyone.

When Mike and Aaron came out of the office a few hours later, I could tell by the look on Mike's face that Aaron had told him something awful. Aaron still didn't want to tell me any details. I told him that I have broad shoulders and that when he was ready, he could just lay it on me. I told him that when he was ready to talk—and I promised I wouldn't push him—I would be ready to listen.

Even now, these years later, he hasn't told me any details. Knowing what little I know, I can only imagine. And it makes me shudder.

Aaron is still angry at me. He's angry that no one noticed—not me or Erin, Mrs. Probst or Mrs. Smith. I don't mind when he takes out his anger on me. Taking things out on me is the safest way for him to express how he feels. I accept that.

8

No One Believes Me

Aaron

When the principal called me the morning after I asked my mom about those sex offender websites, I was worried. I knew what was coming. They took me to the guidance counselor's office and the head principal was in there, too. Both were women—Mrs. Probst and Mrs. Smith—and they asked me if I knew why I was there. I said that I didn't. They said that my mom had some concerns about me, that she was worried something was going on with me. They asked me if everything was okay at home. And I said it was. Then they asked me again if I was sure that everything was all right. And I kept saying that everything was okay. Then they said they were going to ask me a question, and I had to try to answer it as honestly as I could: Did someone do something to you? Is anyone hurting you? That was when I just couldn't take it anymore. I broke down and cried and said yes.

They asked if someone was hurting me sexually and I said yes. When they asked who it was and I told them that it was Jerry Sandusky, all the color went right out of their faces. I wouldn't give them any details, because it was so embarrassing to tell that kind of stuff to women. I felt like a woman might think that I was gay, and I didn't want women to think that about me. With a

Aaron at fourteen, the same year
he spoke up about the abuse

man, I could talk about that kind of stuff and a man would understand how a guy like me would feel. A woman wouldn't get it.

Since I've spent time in therapy, I'm getting myself to understand that what Jerry did to me has nothing to do with being gay; it has to do with abusing children, and that's it. At the time, though, I was confused about so many things, that one included.

The school called my mom and told her just that she needed to come down to the school right away. Mom was there pretty fast, and when she came flying into the room, Mrs. Probst and Mrs. Smith made me tell Mom what I told them. Mom was frantic. She wanted them to call the police, but they wouldn't. They actually told her that we both needed to think of the ramifications of what I was saying. They said that Jerry Sandusky was a man with a heart of gold and he would never do anything like what I said.

I was crying. I was extremely upset and kept saying what I had felt all along would happen if I ever told: "See? See? They don't believe me." I must have said that a hundred times.

When Erin was driving my mom and me to Children and Youth, I doubted that anyone there would believe me, either. It was my word against Jerry Sandusky's.

I was sure that no one would ever believe a kid like me.

Then I met Mike Gillum.

9

How Do You Mend a Broken Boy?

Mike

Children and Youth Services has a major presence in the county and I've worked with them for about ten years. Until Aaron came into my office that day, I thought I'd seen it all. Often in situations of both domestic and child abuse—whether sexual or physical—victims come to us first, even before they call the police. We have intake workers on the ground floor who meet with the people and take a statement, and then we go from there—filing reports, alerting the police and local district attorneys.

Karen Probst had followed procedure and alerted us at CYS that a boy and his mother were on the way to see us with an alleged complaint of child sexual abuse. She called when they were on the way, rather than before they left her office, which was usually the protocol. When Aaron first got to us, he met with Jessica Dershem. She's one of our CYS intake workers who evaluates cases like this and gathers information. Aaron gave her some, but it was clear to her from the start that he was far too uncomfortable to say what exactly had happened, although he did indicate that there was a problem with a guy named Jerry Sandusky.

Jessica is a young woman, not a sports fan, and didn't recognize Sandusky's name. All she knew was that the boy in front of her was far too distraught and completely reluctant to open up to her. Sometimes a kid will come in and he's beaten black-and-blue and won't tell who the perpetrator is. I'll see the child when the intake workers can't get him to open up. This was the case with Aaron. Of course, with Aaron, there were no physical signs on his body, but the look in his eyes was enough to tell me what I was dealing with. What I didn't know was the enormity of the situation—not in terms of who the perpetrator was, but in terms of the prolonged and brutal nature of the sexual abuse.

Before she called me, Jessica called our director, Gerald Rosamilia, and said she had a most reluctant fifteen-year-old boy in her office who wouldn't offer any details of sexual abuse beyond some fondling. Given the boy's distress, she felt there was more to the story. Then she told Rosamilia that the alleged perpetrator was a guy named Jerry Sandusky. Although Rosamilia didn't say too much to Jessica in that moment, later he told me that he recognized Sandusky's name immediately. That was when he told Jessica to have him talk to me. Rosamilia felt that I might be more successful in getting information out of the boy. It didn't matter to Rosamilia who the perpetrator was. He has been with CYS for about thirty years, and he's a strong advocate for children.

The county brought me on as a contractor for CYS in 2005 because I had an excellent reputation in terms of working with kids—not just successful in treatment, but in getting them to communicate. Most kids are reticent to talk about abuse, sexual or otherwise, and they are reluctant to name the perpetrators. My job is to help them through that.

Rosamilia called me and said that a boy was coming up to see me who said he was a victim of sexual abuse at the hands of Jerry Sandusky. Rosamilia asked if I knew who Sandusky was. I confessed that I only knew that he was the former Penn State defensive coach and that he was associated with the Second Mile.

Other than that, I didn't know a great deal about him. I also said that I didn't know of any association that Sandusky would have in Lock Haven, which was where the boy was from. Jessica had told me that Aaron was a student from Central Mountain High School and that the mother had been to the school, but there were some issues there when the story was told to the principal and guidance counselor, and that's why Dawn and Aaron came to CYS.

Aaron was on the first floor with his mom and my office is on the second floor, so I went down to get him. He was wearing a plain shirt with short sleeves and an unbuttoned short-sleeved shirt over that, even though it was November and far from warm outside. He had on a pair of raggedy jeans and some beat-up sneakers. His blond hair was scruffy and on the longer side and he just looked disheveled, but it wasn't the way he was dressed that stunned me. He was so extremely anxious and moving around a lot, pacing the floor in a really tight area in the lobby outside Jessica's office, but looking down at the floor. His agitation was so high that he was wringing his hands. When he finally made eye contact with me, I could see that his eyes were so red-rimmed that they almost looked bloody. It was obvious that he had been crying. Jessica told me that he was almost fifteen, but he looked younger to me. More like thirteen, and very thin. He was about five foot eight and ninety pounds. He was a slight, small, and very frightened boy.

Dawn was standing right next to Aaron as he paced; her friend Erin Rutt was also there, and both women seemed frantic. They were very verbal with each other, although I can't recall what they were saying. As I approached, their conversation died down. Jessica introduced me to all three of them. Then Jessica looked at Aaron and said that she promised I wouldn't bite, but maybe it would be good for Aaron to come upstairs and talk with me because I'm a psychologist.

Dawn and Erin asked if they could come with us and I said

they were welcome to come upstairs, but I wanted to have Aaron alone in my office. Dawn was not happy about that, which was understandable. Dawn wanted to know when she could talk to me but I explained that I was going to talk to her son first. Dawn was desperate to know what happened and I just kept assuring her that we all wanted to know, and that it was my job to find out. I promised that I would take care of her child.

I rescheduled all my cases for that day because I knew that Aaron and I were going to be with each other for a while. I was not rushing that boy out of there. I knew that often in cases of abuse, we need more time than the usual hour. I walked Dawn and Erin to a separate waiting area near my office, but they followed us down the hall to my office anyway. The whole time I was in there with Aaron, they were walking back and forth; I could hear their footsteps in the corridor. I'm accustomed to ambient sounds but I wondered if Aaron heard them. He didn't appear to be distracted. He was very focused on me. I was a little concerned that they were listening at the door, but I understood because they were extremely anxious. Later on, they said they were jumping out of their skins because they both felt they had missed something that now, looking back, seemed so obvious.

Aaron sat down in a chair, and I didn't sit behind my desk, as I would typically do. I pulled a chair around and sat next to Aaron like you would in a sitting room.

I knew this was going to be a tough one, but I had no idea how tough. I wanted Aaron to get a sense of unconditional and positive regard from me. I didn't want him to think I wanted anything from him. I wanted him to know that I really cared—and I did. I looked him in the eye even when he wouldn't make eye contact and I reassured him.

"I really think I know what you must be going through even though you can't tell me. I've been doing this for a long time," I said. "You know, if someone hit you and broke your arm, or someone touched you in your private parts, well, that's really embarrassing and hard to talk about because you're probably very scared. You're probably so scared that if you would say who it is then whoever that person is will be really mad at you, right?"

He barely nodded his head.

"It's my job and purpose to protect you and help you," I said.

The first thing that Aaron said was that no one at the school believed him and no one ever would.

I told him that I believed him. "You know, I've seen kids in situations where they're hurt and it's by someone they care about. I'm not here to take kids away from someone they love, but if someone they love has a problem with anger and they do things that they shouldn't do, I want to help that person as well. Our goal is for families to live together—but happily and safely. It's not always parents who are involved. Sometimes it's a stepbrother or the guy who owns the neighborhood store or even Mom's boyfriend. I'm here to help the kid through it. Whatever happened to you, I believe you."

That usually gets a kid to acknowledge if I am anywhere close to what the situation is with regard to their fear and what they're going through. If I'm lucky, they just acknowledge spontaneously without too much prodding. Sometimes I have to keep asking if they're really scared, and I'll then ask questions like, "Is it more like this: Someone you just met? A stranger? Someone that you know and see every day, like in your house or outside?" It's like that old kids' game of Hide the Button, where the kids say yes when you get closer and no when you're just on a cold trail. I don't want kids to feel threatened, because this way they don't betray their abuser, and that's a common fear among victims. Although they give me information, they don't feel held accountable because I'm guessing, but my guesses are educated. It's clear to them that I'm guessing well. I reassure them that I'm not going to run and tell people what they're telling me. I assure them that I can keep a lot of things just between us—but if someone is hurting them, I have an obligation to do something about it.

At first, Aaron seemed frozen with fear. There was no disarming him and he was too old for me to distract him with some of the toys I keep in my office for little kids so they can act out what happened. It wasn't easy for either of us that first day.

With Aaron, I was more serious about conveying that I was on his side and that I was going to take care of him 100 percent. I told him that I understood his dilemma and his fear—and his predicament.

Aaron still wasn't talking.

I kept my body language open and I just said, "Look, I know that something terrible happened to you. I understand that you want it to stop and you want to get away from him and you're not sure if you want to take it any further than that."

At that point I knew that Aaron just wanted out of the situation. I knew that Aaron, like so many other victims of sexual abuse, was afraid to take it further and press charges or get anyone arrested or make anyone angry at him. He just wanted out.

Aaron was beginning to open up, not in words, but his body language relaxed some. Though I knew he was fifteen, I couldn't get over how young he looked—and his mental function and maturity appeared to be that of a twelve-year-old as well. This is typical with victims of crimes and sexual abuse. Development becomes arrested when the abuse begins.

He acknowledged that he was reluctant to talk about anything, and I kept acknowledging that I understood that. He was very nervous. He finally admitted that the man had touched his genitals and kissed him on the mouth, and he was painfully uncomfortable as he told me. He said there were more details that he just didn't want to talk about right yet, but that he would in the future. He also said that he did not want anyone female to know about what happened to him. Especially his mom. He didn't want her included in any of the meetings or to be privy to what had happened to him. He also said that he had a girlfriend and that was another reason he didn't want anyone to know what had happened to him. He didn't want anyone to think he was gay. And then he pleaded with me to keep Jerry Sandusky away from him.

I assured him that I wouldn't tell any of the details to his mother. The whole time I was with him, I wasn't really taking notes, even during that first session. I wrote my notes up afterward. I did write down some trigger words, though. I explained to him that I had my own shorthand for things that prompt my memory because I would have to write things down later. I knew that taking notes would make him uncomfortable. I also wanted him to feel that he had my full attention. He was with me for a couple of hours before he told me that oral sex had occurred. Even then he didn't tell me on his own; I asked him and he said it had.

At first, when he talked to me about some of what happened, he didn't react as though the behavior was as deviant as it really was. That was because the abuse started when he was so young. If the abuse had started when he was fifteen, he would have been outraged. At fifteen, a boy understands sexual boundaries. Aaron, having been a victim beginning at the age of not quite twelve, and having been groomed since eleven and abused for so long, didn't understand how abnormal the acts were.

We were together for nearly three hours that day, and finally he became more like a fifteen-year-old and the notion of boundaries had kicked in. In the subsequent sessions, he admitted that he was concerned about the acts escalating to anal intercourse. He was finally digesting that the things that happened to him were wrong. I was very blunt with him when I asked questions but gave him the ability to answer with a yes or a no, and that relieved him of a lot of burden.

I didn't focus on the perpetrator in that first session. I only focused on Aaron and what happened to him. I wanted to make sure he wasn't suicidal and that his needs were fully met by me. I also wanted to ascertain whether he needed medication, because his anxiety was so acute and significant. I did not feel that he was at risk, but I knew that his anxiety level was high and I had a feeling it would only increase.

After he confided in me, stating the nature of the abuse to the best of his ability, I explained the process. I said that Jerry Sandusky would ultimately be arrested because what he did was a crime. When Aaron heard that, he kept repeating that he was afraid that Jerry Sandusky would have him killed. Assurance for his safety and his family's was of the utmost importance to Aaron.

In no way at all did I think he was paranoid. Even at that point, before I realized the power of his abuser, I felt that fear was justified. All kids are terrified in cases like this and the extent of Aaron's abuse was enormous. Of course, once I understood the perpetrator's identity, his fears seemed even more valid. Aaron was matter-of-fact when he spoke of Sandusky's power and said that Sandusky could easily hire people to kill him and his family. I assured Aaron that CYS could provide safety. I explained that we worked with law enforcement and sheriff's deputies who were right there in the building at CYS. And we could make arrangements to make sure he and his family were safe at home as well. I told him that we would alert 911, and that if he saw or heard anything suspicious, 911 would make sure that a patrol car would come immediately. We'd even step up patrols in his neighborhood and around the school.

I tried to rationalize with Aaron and said how it would be foolish for Sandusky to attempt to harm him, because Sandusky was going to deny it all. If he tried to threaten or harm Aaron, it would appear to be an admission of guilt. Aaron was able to process that a little bit. To some degree that calmed him.

His secondary fear was a concern for Sandusky. Aaron was a sweet kid, and like so many abused kids, they're concerned about their abuser. He asked me very detailed questions about if Sandusky went to prison, how long he would be there. He worried that something bad would happen to Sandusky and said that all he wanted was to get away from him. He wasn't looking to punish him. He actually felt a little guilt when it came to Sandusky as well: Here was this man with whom he had been close and now he was going to be punished. This is also very common among children who are victims of pedophiles. Like Aaron, the abused child is often confused as he tries to sort out who exactly the perpetrator was to him: A best friend? A father figure? A predator? On one hand, Aaron was worried that Sandusky could kill him. On the other, he was worried that Sandusky could spend his life in jail. The conflict he felt appeared to be overwhelmingly intense.

At the end of that day I promised Aaron that I would be with him throughout this whole ordeal. I said I would see him through from beginning to end and meet with him every day if that's what it would take to make him whole again.

10

Trying to Trust

Aaron

JERRY STOLE A LOT OF THINGS FROM ME—BUT MAYBE MORE THAN anything he took away any kind of trust that I had ever placed in anyone. To this day I'm still working to get that back.

The day that Mom and Erin took me to CYS, I didn't trust anyone. I had just come from the school and they didn't believe me. I couldn't tell any of my friends what was happening, so there was just no place to turn. But even at the school, when I told them what happened, they looked at me as though I was a liar. Some crazy mixed-up kid who was making up stories about a great man.

People let me down. People didn't believe me.

So when my mom and Erin went with me to CYS and I met with Jessica, there was no way I was going to tell Jessica anything. I wouldn't open up to her because she's a woman, even though my mom and Erin weren't in the room. So Jessica brought me to Mike. The truth is, I only agreed to go to his office because I wanted Jessica to stop asking me questions and she said that Mike was the alternative since I wasn't answering her.

I was shaking and crying. Mike pulled out a chair for me and pulled one up next to mine. I looked at him. He's a big, burly guy with a thick head of hair and a mustache, and even though I didn't trust him one bit, he put his hand on my shoulder and said, "Hey, let's just talk a little bit. I know you're really upset. Let's just hang out and everything's going to be okay. I'm on your side."

I'm on your side.

That first question Mike asked—did something sexual happen to me and who was the abuser—was huge for me. Right then, I felt that Mike knew that I wasn't just a boy who lodged a complaint. This guy believed me right from the start.

Even so, Mike didn't really know yet what was going on. All he knew from Jessica was that something might have happened between Jerry Sandusky and me. But he didn't seem to care who this Sandusky guy was; he seemed to only care about me. That was a start. Mike knew there was an allegation of abuse but he didn't know the nature of the allegation. He knew that I said I had been hurt in some way but he didn't know how.

So there's Mike saying all the right things and I know he's the psychologist at CYS and I actually found myself trusting him just enough to open up the slightest bit. I told myself that my instincts were way better now than when I was twelve. I was so upset about not being believed, and I knew that if I told someone who had the power to make it stop, then maybe they could keep Jerry Sandusky away from me. So even though I didn't trust Mike completely at first, by the end of that first day I figured he was a 6 on a trust scale of 1 to 10.

It was what Mike said to me after I began to open up to him a little that built up the trust. As long as I told him that something happened, I didn't need to go into any detail. I just needed to tell him if something sexual happened, like touching or oral sex, and he would ask me so all I had to do was say yes or no. He was real straightforward. When I said yes, that oral sex happened, Mike just said that I didn't have to talk about it more right now, but at some point, when I was ready, I could talk to him more.

As I began to open up over the hours and days and months and years, Mike kept explaining to me what Jerry's MO was. What the MO is for all guys like Jerry. Mike just kept saying that Jerry was the exact profile of a predator. When it finally sank in, I felt angry. I also felt extremely stupid because I didn't catch on. When I told that to Mike, he said I was being way too tough on myself. I argued that I never should have let any of that stuff happen to me. Mike explained that I was a child when it started and it wasn't my fault.

In the beginning, I was more afraid of Jerry than I was angry at him. Like I said, I was angry at myself for being such a stupid kid—but when it came to Jerry I was petrified for a long time. As time went on, things balanced, and although I was still angry at myself, I was angrier at Jerry. I was also angry at other people who I felt let me down, like Mrs. Probst, Mrs. Smith, and, maybe the worst of all, Coach Steve Turchetta. He was the athletic director, the football coach, and the assistant principal at my high school. Jerry called him whenever he wanted to pull me out of class and Turchetta just handed me over. Jerry was the assistant volunteer coach for the football team, and I didn't even play football, so didn't Turchetta wonder *why* Jerry was pulling me out of class?

If that wasn't bad enough, just a couple of days after Mom and I went to CYS and made the report, my mom was shopping at the Goodwill when a woman came up to her and started screaming that Mom and I were *disgusting* for what we were doing to Jerry. Now, the woman was no stranger to Mom, who had grown up with the woman's kids. Still, Mom said the woman acted like my mom was an outsider and told her that the charges would never stick and he'd be back at the school before we knew it. One of the woman's grandkids played on the football team and she said that the parents of the team members were angry that Jerry wasn't allowed to coach anymore and they knew it was because of what I said about Jerry. She also said that people didn't believe me and that Mom and I were lying because we hoped to get money out of Jerry in a lawsuit.

When Mom told me what happened, I couldn't believe that people in my town violated my privacy and talked behind my back. How could they say I made up this story for money? I felt so betrayed. Kids are supposed to be able to trust adults like neighbors, teachers, principals, and coaches. When I told Mike what happened, he comforted me. He told me to just hold my head up high and keep moving forward. He said he was going to make sure there was justice. Without him, I think I might have hit rock bottom.

I saw Mike every day for weeks and I called his cell whenever I needed him. I still see him every week and he's still always at the other end of the phone. That chair where I sat that first day is the same chair I've been sitting in now every week for the last three years. It's in that chair and with Mike in the room where I feel the closest thing to trust that I can feel.

11

The Writing on the Wall

Mike

It wasn't until I had met with Aaron at least three or four times that I realized who we were up against. Sandusky wasn't your ordinary perpetrator.

After about four sessions with Aaron, I had a meeting with Rosamilia and Jessica to report my overview of the case. We were embarking on the initiation of the paperwork and summary to the State Office of Children and Youth, and issuing a report to the Pennsylvania State Police stating that child abuse had occurred. This was all standard operating procedure.

On the civil side, CYS can indicate a level of guilt. That's what we call it—"indicate." We can find, based upon our evaluations, that someone is guilty of child abuse; once an individual is indicated, that individual can no longer hang out with children or be in a job where the individual works with minors. An indication means that we have identified a level of guilt even though the perpetrator hasn't been criminally tried. On the criminal side, there is the district attorney, the local police, or the Pennsylvania State Police, but as an agency, if we at CYS believe that someone is guilty, we have the power to contain them.

We got that indication in motion, and after a letter went out to Sandusky stating that he was indicated, Rosamilia discontinued CYS's informal relationship with the Second Mile. Rosamilia was convinced that Sandusky was guilty of abuse when it came to Aaron. There was no doubt in his mind or mine that the evidence Aaron presented supported his story.

By this time, I knew that Sandusky was the founder of the Second Mile, and although I knew about the camp and I knew that CYS often recommended children to the camp, there was a lot I didn't know until later. Unlike me, Rosamilia knew exactly who Sandusky was, the power he held, and the power of those around him. I just knew that he was a former defensive line coach who had retired and founded the camp; that was about it. Unlike a lot of people in my town and in the state, although I was a Penn State fan to some extent, I was never quite the fanatic. I was never that entwined in the culture and mystique of Penn State.

It wasn't until the end of November, after Sandusky had been indicated by CYS, that Rosamilia and I had a real heart-to-heart. Rosamilia told me that not only had Sandusky founded the Second Mile in 1977, but he was more than a figurehead. He was extremely active there and worked directly with all the kids.

Aaron told me that Sandusky also volunteer-coached at his middle school, and when he entered the high school, Sandusky positioned himself as a volunteer football coach there as well. It was Aaron's feeling that Sandusky wanted to be closer to him. Once he was in high school, Aaron stopped playing football, mostly because he didn't want to be around Sandusky, but Sandusky stayed on anyway.

I knew that the teachers, principals, coaches, and school superintendent were all friends. Everyone knew their relationships extended socially beyond the school. This is a small town, and people talk. In light of the school's deplorable response to Aaron's complaint, I felt that the school was also rife with favoritism when it came to Sandusky.

Not long before my sit-down with Rosamilia, Aaron told me

about Dawn's run-in with the woman at Goodwill and that people in town knew Aaron's identity. Who would have the audacity to divulge a child's name? Especially a victim of sexual abuse. What a betrayal on so many levels. How could friends and neighbors dispute Aaron's allegations and then slander Dawn and Aaron by saying that they manufactured the story in the hopes of getting financial compensation? I really had to keep my cool as I counseled Aaron.

Here was a kid who was a star athlete, never in trouble with the law, didn't drink, didn't use drugs, was just a really good kid, but now condemned by at least a portion of the community. Far too many were beguiled by Sandusky.

I wondered what would have happened if Aaron had been the son of prominent and affluent parents, instead of a kid who lived in public housing and whose single-parent mother relied on welfare. I felt that Aaron was being discriminated against because his family didn't have means. I believed that the case would have been handled differently and the community's stance would have been more sympathetic if Aaron came from a different background. I was getting pretty worked up as I pictured an alternate scenario with well-heeled parents. I figured they might have hired a private attorney and simply snuffed out the ugly allegations. Since Sandusky was the accused, the family might have just swept it all under the rug to avoid the spotlight of public scrutiny. Or maybe their reputations might have been at stake if people said they didn't do enough to protect their child. Or maybe they would have preferred to suppress all of it to avoid the stigma of child sexual abuse. For sure, their kid would never have come to CYS and I wouldn't have counseled him. My imagination was off to the races, but I didn't think it was unrealistic.

The notion that people challenged Aaron's credibility enraged me. I calmed myself by thinking that maybe things happen for a reason. Regardless of a family's economic or social status, a kid still needs counseling after a trauma like Aaron's, and CYS and I went to bat for him legally and therapeutically. Maybe if this had happened to a kid who was from a notable family, Jerry might still be at the school, tooling around the Happy Valley, and running the Second Mile. My focus needed to be solely on Aaron's state of mind and getting justice. As Rosamilia and I traded information about Sandusky, a bell went off in my head. Was the community's questioning of Aaron's credibility spawned from small-town gossip and politics, or from something more sinister?

The second bell went off when Rosamilia and I were talking about Sandusky's retirement from Penn State in 1999. We both just looked at each other. The guy was in line for Joe Paterno's job as head football coach. Everyone was talking about the fact that Jerry Sandusky would be JoePa's replacement if he ever stepped down. So, why would Sandusky retire? There were no reasons given for illness or family problems, just that he was devoting more time to other pursuits. So, did he retire or was he forced to retire? Then Rosamilia said that it was strange that even though he had been a shoo-in for Paterno's coveted job, Sandusky still remained a fixture at Penn State with dinners and fund-raisers—and of course, the Second Mile Camp, which was billed as a salvation for every underprivileged or compromised child in the state of Pennsylvania.

We were thinking the same thing. If you're so active at the college and at all the fund-raisers and the charity gigs, why retire when you could have been JoePa's successor? What happened in 1999 that made Sandusky retire, and did he really retire or was he asked to leave? Rosamilia said that after 1999, Sandusky retained professor emeritus status, got a sweet retirement package, and still maintained an office on the grounds of Penn State given his affiliation with the Second Mile. So, again, what happened in 1999?

We talked back and forth and mulled it over, then we both said out loud, "Who are we up against?" In that moment, we both knew: We were just a human services organization and Sandusky knew everyone who was anyone.

We took care of all the "nobodies" who would otherwise be lost in a system. Rosamilia and I had been doing this kind of work for years and years, and although this wasn't unfamiliar territory for either of us, we had never dealt with anyone like Jerry Sandusky in terms of that level of celebrity and power. Most of our perpetrators are family members. Once there was a teacher, but nothing on the level of Sandusky. Within the confines of the state of Pennsylvania, this was like a kid saying that he was abused by the president of the United States. Sandusky had celebrity status, money, power, and resources way beyond what we had at CYS. But Rosamilia and I agreed that we would follow through on this no matter what. We both knew that the job fell to me as Aaron's psychologist.

The bottom line was that I was more than convinced that Aaron wasn't the first of Sandusky's victims. I was also determined that he would be the last.

Part II

Building the Case

12

Chains of Command

Mike

THE FIRST THING I DID AFTER THAT FIRST MEETING WITH AARON was talk to Dawn. I told her that we needed to move ahead with this and that I needed to see him the next day and quite intensively for a while. That was fine with her. She was grateful.

Rosamilia and I hadn't had our first heart-to-heart yet when I made my first call to the principal of Aaron's school, Karen Probst. I told her who I was and what the situation was and stated that Jerry Sandusky was now under investigation for child abuse. I then stated in no uncertain terms that he could not be on the campus of her school. Under other circumstances, Jessica could have made that call. I made it personally, however, not because it was Jerry Sandusky but because the abuse was beyond the pale. It seemed to me that Mrs. Probst was taken aback, even though she knew that Aaron had been in her office that morning. She hesitated, then said, "Okay"—and that was the end of the conversation. It was what she didn't say or ask that struck me. She didn't ask what the nature of the abuse was. She didn't ask for details. She didn't ask if Aaron was all right or if he would be in school the next day. I also thought it was strange that she didn't explain why she and the guidance counselor had sent the boy

home and not taken his account more seriously. Was it because
Aaron's allegations were so inconceivable when it came to the
man he accused?

The entire scenario was altogether peculiar. Dawn was so
distraught and said she had begged the school to call the police
or some other agency, yet the school had refused and said to
"sleep on it." This was not the typical protocol with this kind
of complaint from a child. Of course, when Aaron came in,
I wasn't concerned with protocol; I was simply concerned
about the distress of the boy. Once I spoke to Mrs. Probst, the
wheels were turning in my head that something was simply all
wrong. I sat back in my chair and thought, *What the hell is going
on here?*

That was when I called Rosamilia. Jessica and I met with
him, and then I met with Rosamilia alone. Little by little, conversation after conversation, more and more pieces started falling
together—although, even then what we put together was only
the tip of the iceberg. The problems we anticipated weren't nearly
as daunting as what was to come. In that first meeting with Rosamilia, although I suspected that Aaron wasn't Sandusky's only
victim, I never anticipated the scope of it all.

Most of all, we knew at that point that Sandusky was a celebrity, but the height and breadth of his popularity and his public
presence still weren't resonating with me. I didn't quite have my
head around the fact that Sandusky was just shy of being iconic.
Yes, he was a big shot at Penn State. And yes, now there was a
question in my mind as to why this man identified by this one
boy as a pedophile had resigned in 1999 yet still ran a camp for
kids. But I know now that I wasn't up to date on Sandusky. Not
even close.

It was clear, based upon Dawn's story and after my call with
Karen Probst, that the school had a relationship with Sandusky
as well. Why else would a school principal and a guidance counselor dissuade a mother—*and dissuade her in front of the child*—

from taking any action? Why did they say that perhaps the allegations were wrong? Why didn't they dig deeper?

Nothing made sense. The more I thought about the school, the more upset and disgusted I became that they would argue in front of the boy and tell him to go home and sleep on it. It's so hard to get a victim of any kind of abuse to come forward, and if you're a guidance counselor or a principal you're expected to be not only professional but empathetic. Given how distressed Aaron was and continued to be, how in the world could they question the authenticity of his statement? He didn't give them details of sexual abuse; he just said that Sandusky had abused him. When they asked him if it was sexual, he said yes. I was extremely worked up by the time I hung up the phone with Karen Probst. I had been doing this kind of work for years and never seen anything like this. Even if a principal had some doubt about what a student was presenting, that's a behind-closed-doors conversation and you are obligated under the law, particularly as a school faculty member or administrator, and no matter what your personal opinion is, to make an immediate report. It's not your call to make in terms of veracity.

Everything seemed backward. The school never even called me until after they learned that Dawn was bringing in Aaron. I knew now that the only reason they called was that Aaron had made a report to them of alleged abuse and the omission of a phone call to us would have looked really bad for them after the fact. They were covering their collective ass.

My mind started going even further. You have a mother and child who are in such distress over this kind of allegation and there is no staff member from the school who *drives* them to CYS? There's no call to either CYS or the police to say that this mother is far too upset to drive and we need assistance? I wrote up the report on Aaron and gave it to Jessica, who is required to file a CY104 form for sexual abuse that goes out to the state police. She also enacted what we call a "child line," which means

that she filed a verbal report with the state police that very afternoon of November 20; she then sent the written report the following day. The report was sent to the Lamar Barracks, which is
the closest barracks to the town of Lock Haven and CYS. In
Pennsylvania, state police stations (or barracks) are located
throughout the Commonwealth, each typically providing cover-
age to a single county. I was a bit concerned because Lamar is the
regional barracks and Aaron had already told me that the crimes
committed against him were in various jurisdictions. He said
that although most of them were committed while he was at Sandusky's house, Sandusky had also traveled with him to Blanchard
Dam, Philadelphia, and across state lines to Maryland. Crossing
state lines with a minor was something else entirely.

I was mulling things over to the point where I couldn't sleep
at night. It was shaking me up as I came to realize that yes, we
were up against Sandusky, but Sandusky was part of a package
and the package might include Penn State. When I was younger,
in my twenties, I lived in Lancaster County, in southern Pennsylvania. That's Amish country, about an hour west of Philadelphia
and a three-hour drive from State College. I had friends who attended Penn State and I'd make that drive and visit them when
there was a big game. I hadn't thought about those days in years.
Talk about school spirit. Going to a Penn State game and having
a tailgater was the best. And Joe Paterno was, without question,
the greatest football coach who ever lived. When I was in my
twenties, it was really Paterno's heyday. It was the mid-1980s and
Penn State was winning national championships. Just about everyone I knew was a Penn State fan, with the exception of the
occasional Notre Dame fan—and Notre Dame was Penn State's
biggest rival. Everything across the state of Pennsylvania was
about Paterno and football—and getting tickets wasn't easy.
They were always promised to groups of alumni, and even they
sometimes had trouble scoring tickets for the games at Beaver
Stadium. People began talking about a new Penn State football

season in the early summer, even before the preseason. Looking back on it, Penn State was like a mythical place, located right in the middle of what was affectionately called "the Happy Valley." You could only get there by car or bus, unless you were one of the lucky ones with a private jet or a helicopter. Even back in the 1980s, before it was built up like it is today, Penn State was like an island filled with bright, young, progressive people, and it seemed that every kid aspired to go there.

Today, the main street that runs through the college is like the heart of some high-end town. People who attended and have moved away remain diehard fans, and the school is very well funded. How many campus towns have several jewelry stores? The fraternity houses have ballrooms and bar areas even though the majority of frat boys are under the drinking age of twenty-one.

I was beginning to realize that Aaron and I (as his advocate) were not about to confront only Sandusky; we could very well be confronting Penn State, which might rally around the former coach. I knew I was getting ahead of myself, but something was instinctively bugging me.

CYS and I had a meeting with the Pennsylvania State Police a few days after my first meeting with Aaron. We gave them the information we had gathered. This might be confusing, but here's how it works: The local police can only cover the city limits of (in this case) the town of Lock Haven in Clinton County, where Aaron lived and went to school. Sandusky lived in State College, in Centre County, which required the meeting with state police since the alleged abuse occurred where Sandusky lived. I emphasized in my initial call to the state police how difficult it was for Aaron to talk about all of this and how it required great sensitivity on their part. Then we had to deal with the question of which district attorney would ultimately handle this case, since so many offenses occurred in Centre County.

The state police responded by saying that they wanted to

schedule an interview with Aaron for December 12, 2008. Typically under this kind of dire circumstance, the interview would have been within a week. The time period was delayed. At this point, I wasn't fully aware of Sandusky's impact. But something was off in my mind. I tried to be calm. It crossed my mind that there was the Thanksgiving holiday coming up and sometimes they're short-staffed during holidays. I told myself that the interview was still within an acceptable time period, but I was eager to get going. It also crossed my mind that the delay might be because of whom we were dealing with as a perpetrator. I wondered if when the state police got the report it had gone through the normal channels. Did it go straight up the chain of command so that maybe someone in a higher position took over? If that was the case, did that person in a higher position take a pause to consider how they wanted to respond?

I tried not to get ahead of myself.

We had the police interview as scheduled on December 12 with no further delays. During that initial interview, the state police did not allow me to sit in with Aaron. The interview was held in Jessica's office; Jessica, as the intake officer, was allowed to be present. However, the moment the interviewers came into the office, there was something unusual. There were two state troopers, not the usual single individual. In addition, CYS usually deals with a regular state trooper, Trooper Patterson, from the Lamar Barracks, who just happens to be a woman. We typically dealt with Trooper Patterson in situations of sex crimes. She's terrific with the kids and families and we know her well. We trust her methods and integrity. Now, instead of Patterson, we had two male troopers—Trooper Cavanaugh from the Lamar Barracks and Trooper Akers from the Montoursville Barracks. They were big guys, middle-aged, and looked like former military. To say that my curiosity was piqued when it came to Patterson's absence is an understatement.

I took Jessica aside and asked if she knew about this. Did she know why there were two troopers and not one, and why Patterson wasn't there? Jessica didn't know. Neither she nor I was informed ahead of time to expect something different. All we had was a date and a time. There was no heads-up for us—these guys just walked in. True, Aaron was not comfortable talking about the abuse with a woman, but I was certain that Trooper Patterson could have worked around his discomfort. I had prepared Aaron as best I could for this interview, telling him of course that there would be one state trooper, that it would likely be Trooper Patterson, and he could trust her. His having to tell his story to these guys whom I didn't know, and on top of that to two of them at once, made me nervous. Aaron was scared and didn't want to tell his story, but we had talked about it extensively and he knew this was something he had to do. I felt terrible that I had prepared him for an interview with a certain state trooper, and I worried about how he would fare. I also wondered if his faith and trust in me would be shaken.

Even more troubling for me was the presence of the trooper from the Montoursville Barracks. It flashed in my mind that maybe the delay in the interview was, in fact, deliberate because the state police were handling this case differently because of who the perpetrator was. Maybe they really were handling it more carefully. I wondered if these troopers were higher-ranking than Patterson, and had been sent in because Sandusky was a big fish, to be handled with kid gloves? Had they had an eye on him for years and now there was finally some evidence to support their suspicions?

The prevailing feeling I had was that indeed, Sandusky could end up getting special treatment because of who he was. I was afraid that law enforcement would point to the fact that they sent in not one but two state troopers to investigate the matter, and that even though they gave it more manpower than usual, they didn't find the kid to be credible and the kid didn't give them enough to go on.

Aaron was with the troopers and Jessica for roughly an hour with the door closed. This was all according to protocol. The fact that I was not sitting in as Aaron's psychologist was also typical, so I had no problem with that other than worrying about Aaron. Since the Sandusky verdict, the state now has a designated center for sex crime interviews at Geisinger Medical Center in Danville, where they have alleged victims tell their story without having any parents or supporters present. The state insists that the child be with a stranger. I don't agree with that policy at all. Does anyone realize how emotionally tenuous a child victim is?

I was pacing around outside as Aaron was interviewed. I knew how reluctant Aaron had been to offer any information to me that first time and how reticent he remained. I was frustrated and thought that this was just another example of how callous and insensitive law enforcement can be in these situations, and how they don't follow psychological recommendations on how to deal with children and adults who are abused, compromised psychologically, or have mental health issues. I was thinking that bureaucracy is so hung-up on chain of evidence and rules of interviews that they discount, minimize, and reject professional psychological opinions.

After Cavanaugh and Akers completed the interview, they introduced themselves to me. I was expecting some dialogue, but then they just left. They didn't offer me anything—such as *we think he's telling the truth* or *he gave us some valuable information*. Trooper Patterson would have given me feedback. These guys were stone cold. They seemed pretty anxious to get going. All they said was they'd get back to me.

Jessica and I talked for a while after the troopers left and Dawn picked up Aaron. Jessica said that Aaron was reticent, as we had expected. He didn't want to talk about anything in detail and essentially just confirmed that there was sexual touching in terms of fondling and kissing on the lips, but he would not go any further even though it was obvious that more had occurred; the "more" that had occurred was written in my report and the troopers were privy to that. Had the troopers asked him about the "more," as I had during my first interview when I asked if oral sex had taken place? Yes they had, but Jessica said that Aaron denied it. They could have asked him the proper questions in the right way to ascertain the extent of the abuse. Even though Aaron's meeting with the state troopers was only three weeks into his therapy with me, my report clearly said that he admitted that oral sex occurred.

There should have been no doubt whatsoever in the minds of those troopers that this boy was a sexual abuse victim. My report also stated clearly that Aaron said Sandusky had taken him to out-of-state hotels where they spent the night in the same bed.

No one from law enforcement got back to me until a few weeks later. Again, typically, I would have heard back sooner than a few weeks although I admit that it can be inconsistent. I made more excuses. I blamed that second delay on the fact that we were now running into the holidays. When they didn't get back to me until sometime in January 2009, I had a sinking feeling in my gut that the chain of command was more like a barbed wire fence.

If this had been any other child, abused by any other perpetrator under the same or similar conditions, the time from intake at CYS to arrest of the sex offender would typically be within two to three weeks. Jerry Sandusky wasn't called in for an interview until January 15, 2009.

All perpetrators are given an opportunity to dispute a victim's allegations, and despite the depth and prolonged history of the abuses, Sandusky was no exception. This was according to CYS protocol. No special treatment. When we heard that Sandusky was coming with his lawyer, Joe Amendola, CYS called our lawyer, Mike Angelelli. We asked Angelelli to sit in on the interview, and Jessica would be there as well as per protocol. The alleged perpetrators in our demographic at CYS typically don't have the means or wherewithal to engage an attorney. Something was already strikingly different about this case.

Angelelli and Jessica filled me in after the meeting, and it became clear to me that Sandusky was a cool customer. Although he acknowledged some basic aspects of Aaron's allegations, he was smug and dismissive. From what they told me, I pictured him swaggering. Sure, he admitted that he cracked Aaron's back; he hugged him and kissed his forehead in the way that you would a son or grandson. He said there was horseplay, for sure, as anyone who was a father figure like him would do, but the notion that anything sexual occurred was ridiculous. He not only denied the fondling and kissing Aaron on the mouth, but he dismissed it categorically. Sandusky went so far as to assume a sympathetic bent to Aaron, saying that the charges were all trumped up and that Aaron was angry with him, although he didn't know why since he'd done so much for the boy. He was disheartened that Aaron was making these false claims since they had enjoyed such a great relationship. Sandusky suggested that perhaps Aaron was angry and sullen because he, Sandusky, had started doing things and going places with other boys and maybe Aaron was jealous.

All in all, Sandusky acted as though he was totally mystified by the entire situation.

I wasn't at the meeting, but when I got the report on Sandusky's interview, I was floored. In all my years I'd never seen someone flip anything around the way that Sandusky did. Basically, he just said that Aaron was a screwed-up kid, and rather than act angry the way other perpetrators do when faced with these kinds of allegations, he just lawyered up and denied everything, seeming almost sorry for Aaron and this fantasy he had evidently created. I knew in my gut that this would be trouble: Sandusky had an attitude, an attorney, and all the power to assassinate Aaron's character and dismiss the allegations. Sandusky struck me as sickeningly arrogant.

I have a private practice as well, but I am the only psychologist for Clinton County. I supervise our employees and intake officers and oversee the various cases where our counselors physically go, for example, into the homes of current and prospective foster parents to make sure that things are going smoothly. We also go into homes where there are cases of suspected child or domestic abuse. In other words, we run the gamut. Once the counselors make their reports, I meet with families and personally do the psychological evaluations to determine whether a situation can be remedied through therapy. I determine whether an individual offender can be rehabilitated. In all my years and in all the situations, I had never encountered an attitude quite like Sandusky's. It was alarming.

It wasn't until later in the case that I learned something about Joe Amendola as well. At the time, I thought it was disturbing and questioned its veracity, but it turned out to be true. I was told that when Amendola was forty-nine years old, he represented a sixteen-year-old girl when she filed an emancipation petition in September 1996. The petition stated that the girl had graduated from high school in two years with a high grade-point average and worked in Amendola's office. When the girl was seventeen, she and Amendola married and she gave birth to his child. After having a second child together, the two separated and then divorced. This certainly compromised Amendola's character in my eyes. There it was again—a power differential: an older and successful man taking advantage of, in this case, a young woman in a sexual nature. Three years later, when NBC's Bob Costas asked Amendola if he would leave his own children in the care of Jerry Sandusky, Amendola said he would—without hesitation. His ex-wife then posted a comment on her Facebook page that read, "Did Joe Amendola just say that he would allow my kids to be alone with Jerry Sandusky?"

Despite Sandusky's nonemotional dismissal of the allegations, despite his arrogance and his explanations that this was

just an angry and jealous boy, another letter went out to Sandusky stating that he was indicated for alleged child abuse. The
first letter was more of a warning and the second was the real
thing. He received that first letter on January 2, 2009. After his
interview on January 15, he was indicated for real: As an agency,
we found him guilty. He appealed, but in February 2009 his appeal was turned down.

The wheels had been set in motion.

13

All the State's Men and Women

Mike

It was a State Trooper Lear who got back to me at the end of February 2009. I was dumbfounded. What happened to Cavanaugh and Akers? Lear was a completely new player. Again, I wondered what the hell was going on and now I also wondered where it was all coming from. *Who was calling the shots?* I wanted there to be one consistent state trooper right from the start so Aaron didn't have to keep reexplaining things. The only saving grace was that I was now permitted to sit in on all the interviews, though I still wasn't allowed to speak for Aaron. I understood that, and the state police understood that my presence was necessary because Aaron was so fragile.

I'd spent quite a bit of time with Aaron after the initial state troopers, Cavanaugh and Akers, had their interview with him. There was a lot of damage control that had to be done. Aaron was absolutely convinced that Cavanaugh and Akers doubted him to the point of total disbelief. I gathered, based upon their demeanor and Jessica's take during the interview, that they pushed Aaron too far and yet not far enough. As reluctant as he was to talk about the situation, his reluctance was magnified tenfold. I needed to reassure Aaron once again with the coming of

Trooper Lear. Although I was surprised that we were about to be faced with a new state trooper, I didn't let on to Aaron. I assured Aaron that this time not only would there be a single trooper assigned to interview him, but I would be there as well. Of course, I had told him before Cavanaugh and Akers's arrival that there would be one trooper and that it would be Patterson. I was concerned about my credibility with Aaron. I also didn't let on to Aaron that having yet another new trooper assigned to a case was totally in contradiction to protocol.

When I asked Lear who he was, remarking that we'd already had an interview with Troopers Cavanaugh and Akers, he said that it was decided that he would be the trooper assigned to the case. I didn't question at the time who had done the decision making. He went on to say that since I was pretty vocal about there being a single trooper assigned to the case, he would follow the case from beginning to end and take Aaron's story from the top. Again, I said that Aaron had already been interviewed by two other guys, and I explained that Aaron was extremely delicate emotionally and psychologically. Why did Aaron have to take his story from the top? Lear seemed prepared for the question and explained that more detail and information were needed. I have to admit that made sense to me. Lear went on to say that he would meet with Aaron at the end of the month or at the beginning of March, and in some ways I thought the more time we had, the better. Maybe as time went by, Aaron would be more forthcoming. If what Lear said was true, that they needed more details and information, maybe by the time of Lear's interview Aaron would not only have revealed more details to me but would be more comfortable revealing them to someone else as well.

When I mentioned to Lear that usually we dealt with Trooper Patterson, he made no comment other than to say that he, Lear, was now the one permanently assigned. Without further discussion or explanation, it was clear, he was directing me off the topic. He actually gave me a little speech about his take on pursuing Jerry Sandusky.

"I don't care who Sandusky is," Lear said. "I'll put the cuffs on anybody."

He had me convinced that Sandusky wasn't going to get any special treatment and I felt good about that, but Lear's enthusiastic pursuit of Sandusky despite "who he was" didn't overrule the need for Aaron to have support in the room. Lear's speech, with all his bravado about justice, didn't throw me off course. I stipulated again that I had to be in the room with Aaron. He agreed as long as I wasn't coaching or prompting.

In the meantime, there was the question of which district attorney would handle the case, since so many of the offenses occurred in State College, within Centre County and where Sandusky's house was located. Aaron lived in Clinton County. It was similar to the jurisdictional question we had with the state police as opposed to the local police. We decided to contact the DA's office in Centre County but hit a wall. Upon hearing and reading the complaint, the DA recused himself. I never learned the exact reason for the recusal. There was talk along the lines of "He knew someone who knew someone who knew Sandusky," indicating a conflict of interest. The reasons were vague, but there was an implication that the DA felt that he could not be objective. Honestly, there was a moment when I wondered whether he just wanted nothing to do with this case because it might prove to be a prescription for professional disaster.

As it turned out, the DA didn't matter. Shortly after a lengthy conversation with Lear on March 12 in which I further emphasized Aaron's fragile state of mind, CYS was informed that the state attorney general's office would be handling the case. That call came in on March 12 as well—the same day that Trooper Lear contacted me. It was all happening so fast: The DA recused himself, we had a new trooper in Lear, and then the attorney general's office stepped in. My attorney general contact was Jonelle Eshbach. She introduced herself as senior deputy attorney general, just a step down from the state attorney general, Tom Corbett, who at the time was in the midst of campaigning for governor of Pennsylvania. Jonelle made it clear that neither DA, in Clinton or Centre County, would be handling the case and this would be a state matter. When I asked her why the case had been bumped up to the attorney general's office, she stated that she couldn't get into it, but there were a number of reasons why. She said again that she would be the individual who would follow through with the investigation. Jonelle was matter-of-fact and said she'd get back to me shortly. No frills. All business.

If I ever had any doubts before that this was a high-profile case, they were diminished now. Still, I had no warning when Jonelle personally called me. Typically, my dealings are limited to the Pennsylvania State Police, municipal police, and a local district attorney or just an assistant district attorney. Suddenly I was dealing with the senior deputy attorney general for the state of Pennsylvania. When I hung up the phone, I thought, *Holy crap, this is even bigger than I thought.* I went right over to Rosamilia's office and he had the same reaction. Rosamilia was trying to analyze why the case wouldn't just be tried in Centre County, but then we quickly concluded that when the state got wind of the situation, they wanted to be certain there were no missteps. The magnitude of the case was undeniable: The state attorney general's office was usually focused on corruption and investigation of police officers, gambling, vice, organized crime. This was the big time.

By the time Lear came into CYS on March 19, 2009, for the interview with Aaron, I was hoping that I'd gotten Aaron to the point where his skin was a little thicker. I assured him again that Trooper Lear was going to be on his side. I didn't mention what Lear said about putting the cuffs on Sandusky because I thought the vision might upset Aaron, who was still afraid of repercussions from Sandusky or his "people." All I told Aaron was that Lear was on the side of justice.

Lear was a younger guy, younger than Akers and Cavanaugh, and pretty animated. Unlike the other troopers, he didn't quite fit the stereotypical physical profile of a state trooper. He was rather slight, was not tall, and hardly had that military demeanor of the other two guys. I was hopeful that maybe because he was younger and less physically overpowering, Aaron could relate better to him. I had also told Lear before he sat down with Aaron how carefully the boy needed to be handled. I tried to impress upon Lear that I realized the importance of eliciting information and details from Aaron, but that he needed to get the information in such a way that was not only gentler but also preserved Aaron's dignity. And Aaron needed to feel that Lear could be trusted.

In retrospect, I should have mentioned leaving out the cuffs line. To my chagrin, it was one of the first things that Lear said. Although it was intended to bolster Aaron's faith in Lear, it seemed to make Aaron retreat. His eyes got real wide and he became very quiet. Lear was trying a little too hard to convince Aaron that he was on his side and went on to say that he didn't care who Sandusky was, if he was guilty, they'd get him, because Lear's sole purpose was to help Aaron.

Despite my pep talk to Aaron, he still had a tough time coming forth in that interview. He was nodding his head yes or no as Lear asked him pointed questions about the nature of the sexual abuse. We needed verbal answers for the record, and it was hard to keep asking him to state his answers out loud. Aaron gave one- or two-word answers about where he was touched and what happened to him, and when it got to the more graphic details of oral sex, Aaron was still reluctant to state any detail in words. He just kept nodding to indicate that abuse—and particularly, that oral sex—had happened, and then he looked down at the floor as though he was ashamed. The interview lasted an hour. Then Lear shook our hands and left. Even though it was a grueling interview just because the subject matter was so brutal, Lear was a bit of a breath of fresh air for the simple reason that he wasn't the standard macho state trooper. He showed compassion to Aaron and kept reassuring him that this case would not be handled with kid gloves because it was Jerry Sandusky and that he personally would seek justice on Aaron's behalf.

Aaron and I both felt a sense of relief after Lear left—relief that the interview was over and a hope that things would proceed the way they should going forward. Since the initial interview with the two other state troopers, there had been a significant lag in time, which concerned us both, and Aaron kept asking me when Jerry would get arrested and put in jail. Although there was a conflict when he heard the "cuffs" remark from Lear, it appeared that Aaron's concern for harm coming to himself or his family was finally trumping Jerry's arrest and the notion of Jerry in handcuffs.

Aaron's fear of harm emanated from a new understanding that a perpetrator like Sandusky was not a rational person. In any situation, a kid fears his perpetrator both during the commission of the crime and after he has identified the perpetrator. In this case, I believed that even though Sandusky's social, political, and financial power was not fully known by Aaron, instinctively, his fear was augmented. Since my discussion with Jonelle and then the analysis with Rosamilia, I knew his fear was justified.

This was not a typical case of abuse. I tried to rein in my own apprehension, what with the appearance of Jonelle, the conversations with Rosamilia, Sandusky's interview with a lawyer present, and Patterson's absence. It was now impossible not to acknowledge the vast power of Jerry Sandusky. When the attorney general's office stepped in, I thought about Sandusky's contacts. About the tons of friends he had in high places, not to mention his connection to Paterno—and his connection to the Second Mile, which meant he'd had access to children for decades. I'd thought about all this before, but this time I felt sick to my stomach. Even now, did I really know who we were dealing with? Even more than before, this time deep in my gut, I felt it: *There have to be other victims.* The more I thought about it, the more I realized how big the victim pool could really be.

Little did I know that this was just the beginning. I was terribly concerned about the power differential between Sandusky and CYS. For sure, we didn't have the influence and power of Sandusky, and here I have this extremely fragile fifteen-year-old boy whom I can barely get to talk to me about the details of the sexual abuse because he's not only traumatized but also scared to death that Sandusky is going to kill him, even by going so far as to hire a hit man.

How would we even have the ability to prosecute a case like this? I knew that if the case came to fruition, it might well escalate into a criminal trial. How would Aaron handle that? He was so intimidated by Sandusky. That's when it really hit me hard that there was a strong probability—not just the possibility I'd entertained weeks before—that we could easily be going up against Penn State as an institution. As I began to anticipate the pushback, I felt extremely small and powerless.

14

Defense Tactics

Mike

I TOLD MYSELF THAT IT WAS A GOOD SIGN THAT THE CASE WAS bumped up to the attorney general's office. The fact that it had gone that far up the hierarchy made it evident to me that my thoughts of other victims—as well as my notion of Sandusky as a serial pedophile—were not off base.

Just days after I spoke with Jonelle, she called again and asked to meet me at the Lamar Barracks, on April 3, 2009. She said that Trooper Lear would be there as well. I was there early, and I got antsy in the waiting room so I walked outside. When she drove up in a white state-issued sedan, I knew it was her and walked over to introduce myself. Just moments later, Lear came outside as well. Later, Jonelle would tell me that she was put off by him. My take on him was that he was just younger than a lot of the other troopers and lacked experience. Jonelle was an experienced prosecutor, and for whatever reason, Lear just rubbed her the wrong way.

The three of us went into a private room inside the barracks and I explained what I thought had happened with Aaron. I told Jonelle precisely what he told me as well as my psychological take on his state of mind, which bore witness to the emotional hallmarks of sexual abuse of a child. Jonelle reviewed everything that I said with Lear, who concurred based upon his interview with Aaron.

Jonelle was intrigued and I also perceived her as visibly shaken by the details and the psychological aspects of the case, but then she deftly switched gears and became totally professional and all business. She explained that the attorney general's office would be in charge of the prosecution. She also said that as time went on, they might involve other agents from their office. She needed us to keep her apprised of everything that was going on in the case and everything had to be kept absolutely confidential. She wanted me to give her any new information that came from Aaron going forward. She hoped he would become more comfortable and discuss in greater depth the details that were relevant to the case. She made it very clear that the standard of evidence required by the attorney general's office before they could even begin to prosecute the crimes inflicted on Aaron had to be far more comprehensive. In that initial meeting, she said that they couldn't prosecute at their level if all we had was Aaron's complaint—especially if Aaron was reluctant to discuss details. So then why were they investigating the case at that juncture?

I liked Jonelle immediately, but after that introductory meeting it occurred to me that although she was genuine, she was very much a part of a machine. She had superiors to whom she had to answer—namely, Attorney General Tom Corbett. I realized that the prosecution of Jerry Sandusky was not exclusively up to her. I had the distinct feeling that Jonelle was indeed concerned that there should be justice, but that she was extremely worried about the fact that the perpetrator was Jerry Sandusky, and because of his ties to Penn State, this had to be a solid case. As time went on and the case unfolded with dozens and dozens of meetings and phone calls, I found out that my instincts were correct. At one point, Jonelle was candid and went so far as to say that they simply needed more evidence because there was a lot of scrutiny based on the identity of the alleged perpetrator.

I wanted to believe that Jonelle was prepared to take Sandusky down. I also felt that she at the very least suspected and perhaps even knew for a fact that Aaron wasn't Sandusky's only victim. She never discussed any other victims or situations in any of our meetings, but she did allude to the fact that it was strange that Sandusky resigned in 1999. We were in the parking lot after our initial meeting and getting ready to leave when she said, "I can't believe this is Penn State–related." Like almost everyone else in the area, Jonelle was a big Penn State fan. Before we went our separate ways, I told her that I was fully aware of how defense tactics worked in these kinds of cases. The defense will say that the victim was coached to say things that didn't really happen. I made it clear to Jonelle that there was no uncertainty that Aaron was telling the truth. I also said that I wanted to interview other boys who had been associated with Jerry Sandusky at the Second Mile—or that she needed to interview them. I said where there's smoke, there's fire.

Although I had a sense of her discomfort, there was still no doubt in my mind that, as I said, Jonelle wanted justice, and she knew I was committed to making damn sure that this guy would not get off the hook because of who he was or because we had a victim who, like most victims, was reluctant to give information. With most child victims of sexual abuse, their information comes in layers. Of course, at that point none of us even thought about the possibility of a cover-up.

15

Nightmares

Aaron

THE NIGHTMARES CAME A LITTLE BIT DURING THE ABUSE BUT MORE so after the abuse ended and I got away from Jerry. Once I started therapy with Mike and began to tell him everything, the nightmares actually got a lot worse for a while. I guess that's because I said out loud what the truth was and the truth was a nightmare. That's when I knew that I had to talk about it more and more and get it all out of my system, if that was ever possible. I also knew that for me to get justice and for Jerry to get the punishment that he deserved, I had to talk about everything, detail by detail. To tell you another truth, I still have nightmares.

Here's the thing about my old nightmares: Normally when you have a nightmare, you wake up in a cold sweat and you know that you had a nightmare and it wasn't real. Well, mine were the kind that I didn't wake up from. They would just go on throughout the night while I slept, and even though I needed to wake up, I couldn't. They were nightmares about what happened to me all those times Jerry was doing things to me and making me do things to him. In my nightmares, I'd see myself running away, somehow getting myself out of that basement by racing up the stairs, but then Jerry would just catch me and do things to me.

I've been a track star and a distance runner since the ninth grade. But even in my dreams, I couldn't run fast enough to get away from Jerry.

After the case started and I met with the troopers and then with Jonelle, I went from nightmares about Jerry abusing me to nightmares about Jerry having people come after me and kill me and my family and take things from me. In some dreams, once everyone was gone, Jerry would lock me away where no one could find me. They were so graphic in detail that even after I woke up I could recite everything that happened and everything that was said; usually you don't remember dreams or nightmares that well. I talk in my sleep, and so I was also afraid to fall asleep for that reason. What if the nightmares came and then I started talking? What if my mom or Katie or Bubby would hear me? That was when I started sleeping on a love seat downstairs in our apartment. I figured with everyone else upstairs, no one could hear me in case I talked out loud in my sleep.

I still feel more comfortable sleeping on a couch because of all the terrible things that happened to me in a bed. I don't like beds anymore. But even sleeping on the love seat, if I woke up at three in the morning because I rolled over and hit the arm, I jumped out of my skin. Then I'd be afraid to go back to sleep. I started staying up late and sleeping late into the morning, hoping the dreams would stop, but they didn't. Once I even dreamed that I was dead and awake at the same time.

Here's the thing—those nightmares were my reality. They weren't just in my sleep. When I was awake, even when I was at school, I was always looking over my shoulder. I'd check the exits to make sure that no one was lurking in a doorway, ready to jump me or take me. I'm still on high alert even though Jerry's in prison. Even now, when I come home from work at night and when I leave for work or whenever, I check the backseat of the car. I wonder if I'll ever stop doing that.

When I was a little kid, maybe six or so, I loved watching the

TV show *Cops*. It amazed me what they could do. Since then, I've always watched a ton of cop shows and movies. From the time I watched that first reality show, I thought, That's what I want to do when I grow up. I want to be a state trooper and sit in my car, kind of hidden on the edge of the highway, checking things with the radar. I think that's awesome. I don't like being radared myself, and that makes me laugh, but I want to be that guy with the radar gun in my car. I like what those guys do. I like that they enforce the law but they're really protecting people. I want to protect people and make sure that things are right and done right.

Since all those interviews with the state troopers, as tough as those sessions were, and everything else that's happened and what I've gone through, now I feel that way more than ever. I want to make sure that people are safe.

16

Everything Changes

Mike

JONELLE, LEAR, AND I HAD A FEW MORE MEETINGS OVER THE NEXT month. It was becoming apparent that in order for the attorney general to build a substantial case with the results we wanted for justice, we needed more evidence. When asked if I thought there were other victims out there, my answer was an unequivocal yes. The problem was that Aaron was not able to identify any of them, nor had he ever witnessed anyone else being victimized. He did have descriptions of some of the boys who were in his group and some whom Sandusky took along on various outings. He also had some names, mostly first names, but those were the only leads that Aaron could provide.

Jonelle agreed: Her instincts also said there were other victims out there. She went so far as to say that Sandusky had made a career of being around children for too long, and given what happened to Aaron, Sandusky fit the profile of a pedophile. But again she made it pretty clear that in terms of Aaron's case against Sandusky, she wanted to build up more evidence. She needed other people, adults and children, to validate what Aaron was saying.

I wondered whether the other evidence was necessary to

strengthen the case on its own merits or more because they needed it to be ironclad to nail a powerful guy like Sandusky. Was that why no one wanted to stick their neck out for just one boy? In my opinion, the attorney general's office and law enforcement in general were more worried about themselves—a lot more than they should have been in a case like this. It was upsetting that everyone I came across in law enforcement seemed to be either an alumnus or a fan of Penn State, and they were all saying, "Okay, you have this fifteen-year-old boy and you believe him, and in your expert opinion you're saying that this absolutely happened, but this is all you've got."

Again, why wasn't this one victim of child sexual abuse enough? Why was Sandusky still at home?

Despite the lack of other witnesses and victims, the biggest factor convincing me that it wasn't an isolated case was the sheer severity of the abuse. The Second Mile camp itself was Sandusky's likely hunting ground. I spoke to Aaron about just that early on in our sessions. I asked him about other boys who might have been abused by Sandusky. Aaron never witnessed this happening to other boys, but he said that yes, there were other boys that Sandusky spent time with. There were other boys who went with Sandusky to Penn State games or to the pool at the off-campus hotel or on trips out of town to see away games. Sometimes there were a handful of boys with Sandusky and Aaron, as there were on that first day-trip to Blanchard Dam, but as time went on the other boys would be taken home at the end of the day and Aaron taken back to Sandusky's house, where he spent the night. After Aaron's second summer at the camp, he often stayed at Sandusky's house on the weekends.

Eventually, Aaron told me in no uncertain words that it was after that second summer at camp, when he was twelve, that the intensity of the sexual acts escalated into oral sex, which Aaron was forced to perform as well as receive. By then Sandusky had Aaron sufficiently groomed and left in a state of being where differentiating normal from aberrant behavior was impossible. With Sandusky's help, Aaron managed to disassociate himself from the grim reality of abuse, as victims do.

I had been meeting with Jonelle and Lear fairly regularly and then Jonelle called to say there was yet another new state trooper assigned to Aaron's case. When I asked why, she basically didn't answer me, saying only that now Trooper Scott Rossman would be contacting us for subsequent interviews. So Lear was out and another state trooper was going to come in and talk to Aaron, who would have to take it from the top all over again.

Bear in mind that in any other case, by this time an arrest would have been made and there might even have been a trial held. There are some cases when a trial is delayed, but in general a trial could be scheduled for anywhere from three or four months to a year from the arrest. Regardless, in a case with this level of abuse, at the very least there would have been an arrest. Sure, one might have negotiations and plea bargaining, but in a case like this, chances are that someone would have accepted a plea bargain or pleaded guilty and waived their right to trial. *Something* would have been done: arrest, jail, probation, bail. This was super-slow motion. The cold truth was that Aaron, as a single victim, didn't matter.

Aaron now had to adjust to Rossman, and he was very upset. He was also angry because what we had been told was not what was happening when it came to Lear pursuing the case to the limits and essentially assuring that Sandusky would be behind bars. Aaron's trust issues were huge—first, from Sandusky's betrayal of him, and then because Trooper Lear had hit some high notes with Aaron, and even though Aaron wasn't thrilled about opening up to anyone, he had made his peace with Lear and could relate to him.

To make matters worse, during Lear's time on the case, Jonelle met with Dawn and Aaron to explain what would happen down the road if and when Aaron had to testify before a grand jury. Although Aaron was reluctant to speak in front of a room filled with strangers, Lear's presence and role as an advocate had bolstered him.

On June 8, 2009, Aaron met with Rossman. I had talked to Rossman a few times on the phone before then. He sounded professional, but also a bit uptight. He was more the image of a traditional state trooper, and he didn't strike me as someone with much of a sense of humor. Not that there was anything humorous here, but Lear had been more personable, especially compared to the first two guys, Akers and Cavanaugh.

It was my same routine when I stressed to Rossman how gentle he needed to be with Aaron. But it's not always easy to do sensitivity training with a state trooper. Bottom line: Rossman was not a sexual abuse officer, nor was he accustomed to dealing with children who are victims of sexual abuse.

I happened to be downstairs at CYS when he arrived and went into the common area on the second floor where juvenile probation officers are stationed. They're imposing as they walk around in vests and with handcuffs hanging from their belts. When Rossman walked into that area, a lot of the staff recognized him, so it was obvious that some of them had previous interaction with him, which I thought might be a good thing. He was talking to some people and then I introduced myself.

My impression from the earlier phone calls was spot-on. He was polite but all business and quasi-military. If there was a poster boy for a state trooper, it would be Rossman: about six foot three, thirty-something, muscle-bound, military haircut, a Navy SEAL–looking guy—square jaw, broad shoulders, buzz cut—the whole deal. The first time that Aaron and I met Rossman, he wore the gray and black state trooper uniform. He's the guy that Aaron had wanted to be since he was about six years old and dreaming of being a state trooper.

I asked Rossman right off the bat what had happened to Lear and if he, Rossman, was going to stay on the case as time went by.

Just as Lear had done, Rossman assured me that he would be the trooper from now on; he apologized for all the changes since Cavanaugh, Akers, and Lear. I was aware that Rossman was from a barracks in Rockview, which is farther away from Lamar but closer to Penn State. I asked him about that but he skirted the issue; he wasn't "at liberty to say" why all the changes had taken place. All he said was that it was a decision made by his superiors and he was sent in by the attorney general's office.

I reminded him to be aware of Aaron's anxiety level and he assured me that he knew what to do. We went to my office, where Aaron was waiting for us.

Aaron

WHEN MIKE BROUGHT TROOPER ROSSMAN INTO HIS OFFICE, WHERE I was waiting, I've got to admit that the thought of telling my story again was driving me crazy. I could tell that Rossman was trying real hard to relate to me, and he shook my hand really strong. When I first saw him, he reminded me of the guys on all those cop shows. I thought, Whoa, this is one big guy. The first thing he said was "So I hear you run track. I'm a sports guy, too."

Like I said, I knew that Trooper Rossman was trying to put me at ease. He started talking to me about lifting weights and all this stuff, like I was a little kid who didn't know exactly what he was doing. But even though he was kind of like a bull in a china shop—like Pap would say—he was a good guy; he just came on a little strong. Then came the time that I had to take my story from the top, and even though the trooper apologized for putting me through that, it took me a good hour to feel comfortable enough to really tell him anything.

The second time that he and I met was a little easier and we spent about two and a half hours together. Mike was there each time and that made a huge difference for me.

The funny thing is, I had a feeling that Trooper Rossman was not comfortable hearing the information from me. He looked tense, and as I gave him more details, he just kept shaking his head like he had a lot of nervous energy and didn't know what to say. He was awkward, but when I got to a point where I would have a tough time, he would try to assure me that it was okay to talk to him. At one point when I was having a real tough time telling him about the oral sex stuff, he said, "You know what, Aaron? Just because this stuff happened to you, it doesn't mean you're gay. You're a kid and it doesn't mean you're going to turn out to be gay." He meant well but that was the last thing I needed to hear. Here was a guy who was just so macho-looking and he's telling me that I don't have to worry about being gay. I *wasn't* worried about being gay. By that point, I'd been in therapy long enough to know the difference between child sexual abuse and being gay. Pedophiles are sexual with kids—period. Trooper Rossman meant well, I know that, but it was just awkward. Like one time when he was trying to be real casual about something that was pretty serious and asked, "Did he ever try to put his dick in your butt? I mean his penis in your anus?" On that one, Mike stepped in and said what he's asking is "Did he ever try to mount you from behind?" He had to help Rossman figure out how to say it.

I understood that Trooper Rossman wanted me to talk about everything that happened with as much detail as possible. He asked me the names of the motels and hotels where I stayed with Jerry and what city we were in and what day and year we were there. I was frustrated because all I could remember was that Jerry made me share a bed with him, and then when I thought back to that, I started to shake. Trooper Rossman kept telling me that he wasn't trying to put me on the spot; he was just trying to get evidence about what this guy did to me and where. He explained that he needed information and details so that eventually the police could call the hotels and get the receipts and times and lengths of stays as proof. What I told him in detail helped.

He also wanted details about my school and when Jerry was there and what were the names of other kids and where did they live and what did they look like. I remembered some but not all; later I found out that Trooper Rossman and some agents in the attorney general's office went out scouring neighborhoods, just like cops do in the movies. They worked a fifty-mile perimeter and as we all know now, they did track down other Sandusky victims and their investigation worked. And yes, I had to talk to more people after that as the investigation went on, and even though I never felt comfortable telling the story, the one thing I can say about Trooper Rossman was that I knew that he believed me. For a kid who wanted to be a state trooper and as someone who still does, that made a big difference for me. I kept thinking how state troopers are all about keeping people safe, and even more when it came to talking to me, they were about keeping kids safe. That's what kept me going.

17

The First Grand Jury

Aaron

THAT FIRST INVESTIGATIVE GRAND JURY WAS IN JUNE 2009. I WAS fifteen.

When Mike, Mom, and I were driving down to Harrisburg for the first grand jury, a part of me thought that maybe I was ready to go ahead and do this. Then, just as soon as I'd get my courage up, I'd get this sinking feeling that I couldn't go through with it and didn't want to testify. I didn't want to explain myself to a bunch of people, a bunch of strangers, women included. I knew it was going to be hard, and I'd start all over again to feel real determined, and then I'd start to feel like I couldn't catch my breath. It was the same up-and-down feeling all the way to Harrisburg. I didn't know what I wanted to do or what I could do. Jonelle asked me if I could do this and I said that I could, and I told Trooper Rossman that I could, but in that car as we got closer, I was scared.

The lawyers didn't tell me too much that first go-round except to answer the questions honestly and truthfully. Mike prepped me and told me what to expect. The three of us stayed in a motel near the courthouse, and Mike had permission to sit in the courtroom with me.

Once we got to the motel, I settled down a little, but the next morning when we were driven to the secret place and taken to the secret room, the whole thing was just freaking me out. I was so shaky, and afraid that once it all started, there was no way I could ever go through with it.

I just didn't want to tell random people who I had never met before in my whole life this story that I never wanted to come out with in the first place. What I had to tell them was so personal. It was hard enough to tell Mike that first time. It was even harder to tell the state troopers, one after the other and over and over again, and then it was really hard to tell Jonelle, because she was a woman, even though I knew that she was part of the attorney general's office and I had to get past all that.

There was no way I was going to let my mom in the courtroom, but she wasn't allowed in there anyway so that was a good thing. That way there were no arguments or hurt feelings; I knew that she wanted to be there for me. My mom knew that I wouldn't say anything to her about what happened. She accepted that. I told her that if you ever find out anything on your own, don't ever talk to me about it. She respected my wishes.

As I remember it, the grand jury was about thirty people and they were pretty much split down the middle when it came to men and women. The moment I saw them, my anxiety level went up even higher. I don't smoke but I did chew tobacco for the longest time, and even though I'd quit a while back, that day with the investigative grand jury, I tucked a little piece of chewing tobacco in the corner of my cheek. It helped me to calm down a little.

I really started to break down that day in the courtroom when Jonelle took me back to the time when I first met Jerry. Even though I'd told the story dozens of times already, somehow in that grand jury room it felt so different and I felt so exposed. When she asked me about the sexual stuff, I just started to cry. That was when we took a break. I went outside in the hallway with Mike and he gave me a pep talk. Mom hugged me and made some jokes.

Here's the thing: Maybe Jonelle did let me know ahead of time, but once I was in that courtroom, I didn't feel she had prepared me for some of things she was going to ask me about, like oral sex. When Mike and I were sitting in the little cubicle during the recess, he said that he knew how horrible it was for me to tell everything to all those people. He also explained that telling the jury what really happened meant they'd most likely indict Sandusky. I got it. If I didn't tell and just fell apart, then Sandusky would go free. Mike told me to remember that the people on the jury and in the attorney general's office really cared about me and wanted to help me, not hurt me. For me, it was hard to believe still that people were on my side.

Before the break, when Jonelle first asked me about the abuse and the oral sex, I had said no. What I meant was "Yes, it all happened," with the "no" meaning that I just didn't want to talk about it. The jury got confused and that's when she called for the break; it was also because I started to melt down. When Jonelle requestioned me after Mike talked to me and I calmed down, I was able to say "yes" but still not without crying. I knew that Jonelle had to ask me everything, but when she was questioning me about what happened, suddenly I was that little boy again in that basement with Jerry Sandusky. She brought me back to it all. I was that little boy who was too afraid to cry or run. As much as I couldn't stand talking in front of those thirty strangers, I guess in a strange way they made me feel that it was safe to break down and cry.

Mike

As it turned out, Rossman was the one who helped us prepare for the first grand jury, which started on June 16, 2009. The exact terminology was "a secret investigative grand jury" and from the moment I heard this was coming to be, I knew that this was an unusual proceeding for a case like this one. Typically, secret grand juries are for high-profile criminal cases. I knew that this case was becoming exactly that, but to the best of my knowledge at that point, there was still only one known victim, and that was Aaron. Of course, I also knew that the reason a grand jury was convened in this case was that the alleged perpetrator was Jerry Sandusky.

I knew that the investigative grand jury had the most power of any law enforcement tool. I also knew that the attorney general's office and law enforcement were hitting a lot of walls in their attempts to interview people. People did not want to speak out. Honestly, there were some people who also spoke to me confidentially and led me to believe that was the case; they were getting reports on Sandusky as they vetted witnesses and employees and tried to identify other children. Apparently, there were other questionable things that happened with Jerry Sandusky over the years when it came to little boys. But when the attorney general's agents and state troopers attempted to speak to employees at the Second Mile and Penn State, they were just shut out. Picture a cop knocking on a door and the person opens it halfway and then says they've got nothing to say and the door slams closed.

Because the accused was Jerry Sandusky, law enforcement wanted to do everything right. In other words, they wanted a bona fide grand jury indictment rather than one law enforcement official arresting Sandusky and then someone cutting him loose because the evidence was either shaky or insufficient. A grand jury indictment wouldn't be questionable. Politically, it would also diffuse any backlash or repercussions that could potentially fall upon a law enforcement agency or individual for an arrest without cause, which could end up backfiring and leave Sandusky a free man.

It was my impression that the grand jury was convened because the attorney general's office had done its homework, despite the fact that doors closed in their faces and Sandusky kept appealing the CYS indication right up until a week or so before that first grand jury met. Maybe it was wishful thinking at the time, but I figured that the attorney general had some other evidence that came out of the investigation that started with Aaron.

It's always been my feeling that someone in Sandusky's camp must have known that a grand jury proceeding was in the works, because shortly after Rossman met with Aaron, Dawn got a call from a guy named "John," who claimed to be with the Philadelphia Eagles organization. John offered her box seats for the season and when she asked why, John said they were placed aside for her and her son Aaron. John went on to say that he knew that Aaron had attended games in the past and he wanted to offer a 2009 full season pass with premium seats. Dawn wisely said he should call her back, and then she called me. I told Dawn to say that she and her son would not be attending games this season. John still persisted. He told Dawn that he could offer them to others in her family. Dawn still declined and then said that perhaps she'd get back to him. When she asked how he came to offer her these tickets, John claimed that Aaron's name was drawn from a list of names entered in a contest.

One Christmas, Sandusky had put together a photo album for Aaron of times they'd spent together. One snapshot was Aaron and Sandusky at an Eagles' game. At the trial, that photograph album was in evidence. As for "John's" offer, it was either a really strange coincidence and the guy was innocent and on the level, or someone put him up to the task of what boils down to bribery. We let it go. We had bigger fish to fry.

The grand jury convened in Harrisburg, and at the request of the attorney general's office, we went down the night before and spent the night at a Red Roof Inn. Dawn and Aaron stayed in one room and I stayed in another. Trooper Rossman met us in Harrisburg. The following morning we were escorted to a secret office and then to an undisclosed location where the grand jury assembled. It was all pretty intimidating. The private lobby was lined with armed security. We all waited our turn while special identification tags were issued to us; then we were taken to another floor, where the grand jury waited.

Aaron did not want his mother in the courtroom and Dawn understood. Aaron, as he said all along, didn't want her to hear the disturbing details of his testimony. In addition, Dawn had not been subpoenaed, so even if Aaron had wanted her there, she would not have been allowed in.

It was all very cloak-and-dagger. Witnesses are secured and isolated from one another so there is no chance of them running into one another prior to giving testimony. To the best of my knowledge, the only witnesses that day were law enforcement. Because Aaron was so distraught, and because of the nature of the crime and the fact that Aaron was a child, the judge allowed me to stay in the courtroom while Aaron gave his testimony. The judge understood that as his psychologist and confidant, I was needed by Aaron as his port in the storm. The judge understood that my presence would enhance Aaron's sense of security as he gave testimony.

As for me, they had my written reports, which the jurors reviewed, so there was no need for me to take the stand. There's a different set of rules for a grand jury than for an actual trial. Jurors are allowed to read things and to have hearsay evidence. Not only were my summaries of Aaron's case submitted, but there were those from the state troopers who had interviewed Aaron as well.

I was seated at the same table with Trooper Rossman and Jonelle. As Jonelle questioned Aaron on the stand, I was positioned in such a way that Aaron and I were really face-to-face as he gave his testimony. It was a tough process for Aaron. After roughly an hour of his testimony, involving more and more graphic detail, he began crying so hard that he was close to collapse and said that he felt faint. That was when Jonelle asked for a recess. He realized that Jonelle wanted him to go into greater detail and although he did acknowledge that sexual abuse had happened, his answers were short and relegated to "yes" or "no" when it came to certain acts. When it came to the "yes" answers with regard to oral sex having occurred, he nodded, and then Jonelle had to prompt him to verbalize so that the court stenographer would have the answer audibly for the records.

As we got into the hallway, Aaron leaned against the wall and started to slide down. I took him into a little cubicle not much bigger than a closet. I asked Dawn to give him half an Ativan, the anti-anxiety medication that his doctor had prescribed for him, but just half because I wanted him to remain completely alert. It was more a placebo effect. Dawn came into the cubicle, and although it was clear that her anxiety level was high as well, she was strong for him. She tried to joke with her son. "Oh boy, Aaron," she said. "I thought you were going to fall down there for a second when you slid down that wall." She was trying to cajole him a little and make him laugh and keep things light.

I told him that he had done a great job in that courtroom and was really brave to give that testimony. I also told him that we had to go back in because the day wasn't over yet.

Aaron got himself recharged and went back and finished his testimony. This time, rather than just accepting "yes" and "no" answers, Jonelle got him to vocalize more graphically about what had happened to him in terms of oral sex. After the break, he was also able to say that the sexual contact happened numerous times. When Jonelle asked him if oral sex had occurred between them more than twenty-four times, Aaron said "yes." He was loud and clear. Then he just put his head down on the witness stand and started to cry again.

After Aaron's testimony finished, we spoke with Jonelle and Rossman. Both of them said what a good job Aaron did on the stand, and Jonelle said how sorry she was that she had to ask him all those tough questions. She explained how necessary they were, and again, she told Aaron how brave he was. Her pep talk made an impression on him.

As Dawn and Aaron were collecting themselves before we left the courthouse, I had a moment alone with Jonelle and Rossman. They indicated that there was some other evidence that they were not yet at liberty to share with me. It was something that happened in 1998. They didn't say anything else, just that when they had the full story, they'd let me know.

Aaron and Dawn drove back to Lock Haven and I headed home as well. I tuned in a classic rock station on the car radio and tried to chill out. Later that night, I was at my desk and surfing the Internet—playing detective, I guess. Googling terms like *prosecutor, Centre County, State College, Penn State.* That was when I came across the name Ray Gricar.

Gricar was Centre County's top prosecutor when he mysteriously vanished in April 2005. I'd remembered reading about the case a few years before, but now that we were so steeped in prosecution, law enforcement, grand jury, and the attorney general's office, the case of the missing prosecutor piqued my curiosity. Gricar's red and white Mini Cooper was found the day after Gricar's girlfriend reported him missing. Gricar had called his girlfriend on a Friday morning around eleven thirty to say he was taking the day off and driving down to Lewisburg, where he liked to shop around for antiques. Ray never came home that day. His girlfriend called him in as a missing person. On Saturday, his car was in a parking lot in Lewisburg—about forty-five minutes from his home in Bellefonte. The car was in perfect condition—no signs of a break-in, and no blood in the vehicle. The only odd evidence was that Ray didn't smoke, yet faint traces of cigarette smoke and ashes were found in the car. Months later, his laptop was recovered from the Susquehanna River. A fisherman had spotted it under a bridge. It was in pieces, with the hard drive removed. Months after that, a woman spotted the hard drive, which was so water-damaged that no information was retrievable.

It was just an old news story. There was no mention of Sandusky in connection with Gricar's disappearance. Not yet.

18

Wiretap

Mike

AARON CONTINUED TO COME IN FOR THERAPY AT LEAST ONCE A week after that first grand jury, and we held several phone calls in between sessions. I had an open arrangement with Aaron and Dawn to the effect that if either of them needed me for whatever reason, they could call at any time—day or night. Often Dawn called on Aaron's behalf, and if I wasn't in session, I took the call immediately. Sometimes, if I was with a patient and couldn't interrupt the session, I had to steel myself from answering the phone and call them back. Their calls were constant, but this was a crisis situation.

On a personal note, the problem was that this was a pending criminal case that I couldn't discuss with anyone. Not with my kids. Not with my friends or with my colleagues. Not even with my wife. There had been cases I'd discussed with my wife before and simply left out names because of confidentiality issues, but this was one that had to stay just with me. The late-night calls and texts were taking a toll on our marriage. I couldn't sleep, my diet went to hell, and I was gaining weight. I admit that this case consumed me. I felt solely responsible for this boy: I asked myself if I was doing right by him. But I was also convinced that there were others like him out there. Maybe, just maybe, Aaron's coming forward would bring the other victims out from behind their shuttered and shattered lives, and Jerry Sandusky would be revealed as the human hazard that he was and put away forever.

Within a few days after Aaron gave his testimony at the grand jury, Rossman spoke to me about doing a wiretap. He wanted Aaron to call Sandusky and try to get him to acknowledge the sexual abuse in a recorded phone conversation. Rossman said, correctly, that the attorney general approved of the plan. I didn't hesitate for a moment when I said that it would be a bad idea. Aaron was still far too fragile for this kind of intrigue. He continued to worry about Sandusky sending hit men to have him killed. Getting on the phone to lure Sandusky into a confession would be too much for him emotionally; I was certain that he couldn't handle making a phone call like that. It was too sophisticated an endeavor. On the psychological side, I was afraid that just hearing Sandusky's voice could set him back in terms of his treatment. I feared it would put an inordinate stress on his mental health, which we were still trying to balance.

Then there's that old expression that bugged me: Just because you're paranoid, it doesn't mean they're not out to get you. Was I worried that Sandusky or someone else would hurt Aaron or his family? At first, I wasn't. Generally, I assure people that nothing like that will happen. I assure them that we at CYS and local police will protect them. I had said that to Aaron and at the time I had meant it and believed it. CYS does have that power. In this case, however, I was beginning to have my doubts. Aaron was afraid because Sandusky had become so angry with him and even physical on those occasions toward the end when Aaron was no longer obedient, and I wondered how deep things went with Sandusky as far as a capacity for violence—and who he might know that could do his dirty work for him.

For sure, Sandusky's behavior broke the norm of the average perpetrator, because the average perp didn't go to a victim's house when the victim got the guts to finally break off contact. The average perp is not bold enough to repeatedly call his victim's mother, call the victim, take the kid from class, and follow a school bus. When the attorney general reviewed the call logs to Dawn's phone, they counted more than 120 calls from Sandusky between January and July 2008. Those were the months after Aaron had the guts to reject him. Sandusky was obsessed. I thought about models of obsessions in various abuse cases and then the threat of death or harm—like when a woman is trying to get away from an abusive boyfriend, husband, or ex-husband and is being stalked. I'd even had threats myself as I tried to empower abused women to get a lawyer and go to the police. I wondered if Sandusky was suicidal, which would mean that his actions when it came to violence against Aaron might not matter to him. I also didn't discount that Aaron might have picked up on other things when he was with Sandusky in terms of his behavior that he either still wasn't able to tell me or perhaps didn't even consciously recall. One thing was for sure: I did not and would not discount or dismiss Aaron's fears; I knew he was entitled to have them.

So a wiretap was just out of the question as far as I was concerned. I made myself clear to Rossman, Jonelle, and then to Dawn, who thought it might be a final way to break the case and prevent Aaron from having to give any more testimony.

Rossman called me back to ask me to reconsider my professional opinion, but I said that any contact with Sandusky could escalate Aaron's anxiety. I also asked him to consider the possibility that Sandusky was suicidal or homicidal. I was emphatic that no good could possibly come of this wiretap. End of story.

But it wasn't the end of the story. Not one week after Aaron's testimony, and just days after my discussions with Rossman and Dawn about the wiretap, I called to check in with Dawn and see how Aaron was doing. Dawn said that she had agreed to do the wiretap. She explained that the police had contacted her and said that if they got additional and certain evidence through a wire-tap, it might mean that Aaron would have to testify less or per-haps not at all in the future.

I was stunned that law enforcement and the attorney general would deliberately go against my recommendations, circumvent me, and go to Dawn. I was angry that they had manipulated Dawn and disappointed that she allowed it, but she just kept going back to their promise that this would be easier on Aaron in the future. When I asked Aaron how he felt about the wiretap, it was obvious that he was caught between me, his mother, and the authorities. He said he was scared, but the authorities talked him into it and his mom said it would be the best thing to do. Aaron said that he was willing to bite the bullet since the police told him that if he could get Sandusky to admit what he did on tape, then he wouldn't have to testify.

No one asked me to be there on the day of the wiretap—for obvious reasons. I wasn't even sure when it was going to be and just happened to call Dawn on June 22, 2009, late in the after-noon to see how everything was. Dawn said it wasn't a good time to talk because the wiretap team was there along with Rossman and an agent from the attorney general's office named Anthony "Tony" Sassano, who announced that he was now involved with the case.

Dawn said their presence stirred up a lot of curiosity in the neighborhood because there was a big truck and no one was dis-creet about hauling in equipment. Katie and Bubby were there as well. I pictured that it must have looked like a scene out of *CSI.*

Aaron placed the call to Sandusky from the landline in their apartment and spoke as instructed. Aaron said, "I want you to apologize to me for what you did to me."

Sandusky responded, "Well, we can't talk about that stuff now."

The entire call lasted no more than one minute. Aaron wasn't able to encourage more dialogue with Sandusky. I wasn't in the least bit surprised. How could they expect that of him?

As Aaron recounted that one-minute call to me, I thought, now that was an acknowledgment from Sandusky. Sandusky didn't say what an innocent man would have said if a call like that came in. An innocent man would have said, "How could you say that about me? Do you know that you're ruining my life? What the hell is the matter with you?" Sandusky said exactly what I would have expected from a guilty abusive husband or boyfriend. His reaction was consistent with the behavior he exhibited that day at CYS with Amendola, where there was no outrage when faced with Aaron's accusations. To me, his words to Aaron on that wiretap confirmed the sexual abuse.

Now eight grueling months without justice had gone by since I first met Aaron; Sandusky was still a free man. Something wasn't right. As a matter of fact, something was terribly wrong.

19

Conspiracy Theories

Mike

OVER THE NEXT FIVE MONTHS, NOT MUCH HAPPENED. IT FELT LIKE the game plan was changing, the promises were false, and now there was yet another player in the attorney general's office. Along with Jonelle and Rossman, there was Agent Sassano. I was making phone calls almost daily to keep up with the case but was getting nowhere. The law enforcement players kept asking Aaron about other boys who might be victims and he was coming up empty. We'd been down that road before. Aaron was traumatized. He hadn't been focused on other boys as victims during the three years that he endured Sandusky's abuse. It didn't even hit him that he was a victim until he was fifteen.

On September 29, 2009, we were notified that Amendola had filed a second appeal to vacate the indication from CYS for Sandusky, but the appeal was once again denied. Except for that, there was just nothing. I was disheartened and wondered if the investigation was going flat, if somehow, slowly and with a hidden strategy on behalf of perhaps even law enforcement, it was just receding back into the landscape. I kept trying to bolster Aaron's spirits as he dealt with his severe anxiety. He anticipated an arrest and hoped that this ordeal would soon be over.

Although I was led to believe that they needed to keep collecting more and more evidence, I also knew that theoretically the first grand jury could have voted for an indictment, which would have meant a warrant could be issued and Sandusky arrested. Despite Aaron's testimony and the evidence, Sandusky still disputed that there was sexual contact. Even when confronted with the names of venues like motels, Sandusky never denied that they had been there together for whatever outing they attended— a football game or a charity golf tournament. Sandusky's answer when asked why they shared a room with only one bed was basically "So what? That was all that was available." He was lying, out and out lying, and I was exasperated. Aaron, Dawn, and I were floored that in the wake of the first grand jury, Aaron's torturous testimony, and the useless wiretap, Sandusky was still not even close to being arrested.

Too much time was passing. We were now approaching a year since that first day when Aaron walked into CYS. Since then, Aaron had met with at least four state troopers and testified before a grand jury. Besides being anxious, he was discouraged, and that old feeling that no one believed him was rearing its head again. It was becoming increasingly difficult for all of us to believe that justice would prevail, but Aaron was the most despondent. He was also confused: If CYS believed him enough to indicate Sandusky, if I believed him, if it was true that law enforcement and Jonelle believed him, then why weren't they making an arrest based upon his allegations? In Aaron's mind, he wanted Sandusky arrested based upon what he alone reported, and then after that the other victims could be found.

From my point of view, Aaron could have been right. He'd come forth; Sandusky could be arrested and then perhaps the fact that one victim had the courage to expose Sandusky as a pedophile would be an incentive for other boys to come forward. I was certain that once news of Sandusky's arrest was splashed all over the papers, the case against him would elicit victims and evidence from all sides. The attorney general's office and law enforcement argued that an arrest strategy wasn't the right prescription. They needed a stronger case.

Jonelle called. According to the attorney general's office, the first grand jury said that Aaron had trouble responding clearly and didn't elaborate as much as he could have or should have. They wanted a second round and hoped it could prove to be more valuable. The second grand jury would convene on November 16, 2009, although with the same cast, since the jury's term had not yet expired. To say that I was frustrated is an understatement. I was glad that Sandusky lost the appeal, but I had assumed that whatever the first grand jury heard would have some weight and lead us somewhere.

Some of the information that Rossman was able to verify was evidence that Aaron was indeed with Sandusky in motels. Rossman had receipts in hand to prove it. Thus other witnesses, such as desk clerks and waiters, might have seen them together. This should have been enough to ensure that Aaron was telling the truth. It was Aaron's word against Sandusky's as to what happened in that basement room, but a grown man taking a boy to motels and hotels reeked of decadence and sexual crime.

Preparing Aaron for the second grand jury go-round wasn't easy.

The first time that Aaron testified, Jonelle would say something like "He then would touch you in a sexual way," and Aaron would answer yes or no. In the second grand jury, the jurors wanted Aaron to narrate the story in his own words. They wanted all the gory details despite the transparent frailty of this boy on the stand.

I was convinced that they didn't really need that kind of testimony, because the jury must have easily voted to indict the first time around in their hearts, yet they wanted another stab at the case to make certain. I was sure that the jury and law enforcement were really worried that if there was even an iota of reasonable doubt, they were going to get in serious trouble, because they were taking on Sandusky and possibly provoking Penn State and the Second Mile. When you got right down to it, what did they have but this one kid? He didn't even have the moniker of Victim 1 yet. There *were* no other victims. I was positive that this second grand jury was a purely political move. How could they possibly think they would get an ideal testimony out of a victimized child?

There is a legal measure called the Angel Act. It is also referred to as the Tender Years Exception to the hearsay rule. In this situation, the Angel Act would have allowed me as Aaron's psychologist, who was privy to the entire scope of the case, to certify need for other testimony modes for Aaron. In other words, I could have testified as though I was the child if I deemed that the child was too fragile and the court concurred. But neither Jonelle nor the grand jury thought that my testimony would be as effective as Aaron's. The grand jury wanted Aaron's words and the details of his sexual abuse narrated solely by him, recorded by the court, and put down on paper.

Aaron was so apprehensive and humiliated that I couldn't conceive of a way that he would be able to describe anything in detail. Jonelle and I gave him some more coaching and emphasized that he had to state exactly what happened. Jonelle explained that she didn't want anyone on the jury to say that she had been leading the witness.

Once Aaron took the stand, Jonelle was true to her commitment for the grand jury. She pushed him a lot harder that second time. To Aaron's credit, he managed through tears to be more of his own advocate and narrator, until he literally collapsed.

Jonelle had called for a break during his testimony when he exhibited signs of untoward stress. He was pale and perspiring. Once outside the courtroom, he sank to the floor. I picked him up and carried him to the bathroom. He started to throw up a little bit and I brought him over to the sink, where he rinsed his face and mouth. Once I got him back into the hallway, Dawn just held him in her arms and stroked his back. We put him back together. Although we thought he would have to testify further, after that Aaron did not have to go back on the stand.

Although Aaron and I were not present for their testimony, we were told that Agent Sassano and Trooper Rossman took the stand that day. That didn't surprise me, and I thought it was probably something that would work favorably for our case.

Now, there were lots of rumors floating around during the time before the second grand jury. People were dropping hints and the courthouse was buzzing that there were "other" witnesses, even perhaps another "key witness." I didn't probe. I knew that law enforcement had been questioning volunteers and employees from the Second Mile as well as people who lived in the towns of Lock Haven and State College. This was, after all, an investigation. At one point when I was standing outside the courtroom before the second grand jury assembled, an official dropped some papers. I could see there was a witness list. I thought I saw the name Matt Sandusky, Jerry's adopted son. I thought that was pretty crazy. Were the papers dropped "accidentally on purpose"? I still don't know.

A few days later I found out that Matt Sandusky had indeed taken the stand. I was later told that Debra Long, Matt's biological mother, had approached the police. I guess the rumor mill had reached her ears as well. As it turned out, Matt took the stand at that grand jury to defend Sandusky. I had wrongly assumed he was coming forward as another victim. I was confident that the attorney general and law enforcement were seeking out boys involved with the Second Mile and any boys whom Sandusky had taken a personal interest in either "rehabilitating or saving." Much like Dawn, Matt's mother was a single mom. Sandusky took Matt under his wing at the age of eleven, when the boy was a camper at the Second Mile. Sandusky assured Matt's mother that he would keep him out of trouble. According to

Long, Sandusky convinced her that she was fundamentally unfit to control her child, not only emotionally, because there was no father around, but also because she was in such dire financial distress. Sandusky could step in and make sure the child was cared for properly. Like Dawn, Debra Long trusted Sandusky, whose reputation was impeccable. Her son all but moved into the Sandusky home. From my perspective, it was all too familiar. Yet Matt defended Sandusky that day.

After the second grand jury, Jonelle assured us that an arrest was imminent. In fact, she and I had a conversation on February 4, 2010, just three months after that grand jury, about how we would handle the announcement of the arrest, particularly with the press. Then a bombshell fell.

The grand jury was meeting monthly to review the case, and law enforcement officials were still struggling when it came to getting information from the Second Mile and Penn State employees who knew Sandusky. The attorney general's office finally subpoenaed records from the Second Mile. They wanted the box that contained everyone whose last name began with the letter S. Jonelle called to say the Second Mile's personnel records beginning with S were lost. Oddly enough, it was the only box that was missing.

It's impossible to express how furious I was when I heard that. It's equally as impossible to convey how maddening that was for Dawn and Aaron. We all felt the Second Mile didn't "lose" it. In my opinion, they conveniently ditched it. And if that was so, then this was a pure case of obstruction of justice. Jonelle's response was more than disappointing. "I know. It's unfair," she said. "But if we don't have that record, then we don't have it."

We wanted that box in the hope that the personnel records contained complaints, although I assumed those would have been scrapped anyway. We were also hoping that they would verify expense reports about trips taken with some of the other boys and other hotel stays, and maybe names of children in groups that were under Sandusky's leadership at the Second Mile.

Still, Jonelle promised that there would be an arrest in the middle to the third week of March. At that point, I was really pinning her down because this had gone on long enough. She said there would absolutely be an arrest unless one of her supervisors stopped the process.

I asked who that supervisor would be.

"You know who my supervisor is," she said. "It's Tom Corbett."

She was right: I did know. I knew that he was the same Tom Corbett who was running for governor.

20

Conversion Syndrome

Mike

As soon as Jonelle said there was a strong probability that an arrest would be made in March, I started to think that Aaron had to be placed someplace safe. Dawn thought that maybe she could take the kids to Virginia, where she knew the territory, or just hide out in some retreat up in the mountains. We had a plan: Gerald Rosamilia had already approved financial backing from the county in the event that Aaron and his family needed to be placed somewhere for witness protection. It was still February and the arrest was supposed to happen in March, so we had time to find a safe haven and talk to Aaron and his brother and sister so they could adjust without fear to the notion of being temporarily in hiding.

I put in a call to Karen Probst, since Aaron was still at Central Mountain High. I wanted to make her aware that with an impending arrest of Jerry Sandusky, there could be some unpleasant publicity issues. I left her a voice mail simply saying that it was urgent for her to call me. Probst never returned my call.

Although Aaron was excited about the impending arrest, and he had been doing fairly well emotionally for some time—really, since the second grand jury testimony—he suddenly started to have some issues. He was steady enough to allow himself to have girlfriends, but once he confided his story to a girl, the girl shunned him. This happened repeatedly with three or four girls. He thought they could be trusted, and when they rejected him, he was left with a great deal of rage. Even among his peers, sexual abuse was one of the last taboo subjects.

March came and I expected an arrest by the middle of the month, as Jonelle promised. When I hadn't heard from Jonelle by the second week, I started to call her frequently—relentlessly, really. I also emailed her, but none of my voice mails or emails was returned. Between Jonelle and Probst, this was really bizarre.

Finally Jonelle called and said that the second grand jury still didn't feel that Aaron's testimony was strong enough to make a case for an arrest. I didn't say anything but I thought to myself that Matt Sandusky's must not have been strong enough, either. As I said, at the time I thought Matt had turned on his adoptive father.

Into the fourth week of March, Jonelle called again and said that the arrest was further delayed. She sounded uneasy as she explained that there was no reason other than that her present-ment summarizing the evidence from the grand jury still had to be approved by her boss. There it was again: Tom Corbett, the guy at the highest level, running for governor.

Don't get me wrong, because I liked Jonelle. But this process was taking way too long, not to mention the two grand juries and the false promises piling up. I couldn't help but feel that she was putting me off, that she was talking out of both sides of her mouth. She had a situation on her hands, hands that were very much tied, and my gut said that Corbett was ultimately the one holding this up. Jonelle wasn't giving me a lot of detail or any solid answers, even when I asked her directly why the arrest was being delayed. All she said was that I had to understand that this case could be as big if not bigger than the Michael Jackson sex abuse case, and that the attorney general's office could really be scrutinized.

Two more months went by. In May, Jonelle said there was more evidence. But there still was no date set for an arrest. When I pressed her for the nature of the evidence, she conceded that there were other victims. So, isn't that what we'd been waiting for? Didn't that make this case ironclad? No, she said, it didn't. The attorney general wanted to be sure there was no room for error and no public inquiry that could derail the integrity of the attorney general's office.

By the time June 2010 came around, I spoke to Jonelle and called her out. Actually, I showed up at her office in Harrisburg because she wasn't returning my calls again and I happened to be in the area for a psychological association meeting.

I just charged in there. And I had done some research. Until I did my digging, I really didn't know any facts about Corbett and his relationship with the Second Mile and Penn State. I was now far better schooled in the Penn State culture and Corbett's affiliations. Corbett was a former member of the Penn State board of trustees, and I firmly believed that as he waged his campaign for governor he was afraid to alienate Penn State fans and alumni— all of whom were his voters, constituents, and campaign donors. I was convinced that Corbett felt that arresting Sandusky would interfere with his chances of being elected; it seemed to me that justice for a victim of sexual abuse at the hands of Jerry Sandusky was being put on a back burner. I even wrote a memo to Jessica Dershem and Mike Angelelli stating that it was my feeling that the attorney general's office was deliberately delaying Sandusky's arrest.

Jonelle had little to say when I called her out and voiced my opinion. But much like what she said in March, she admitted that her hands were tied. She protested that if her boss wanted to prolong the investigation, there was no way that she could stop him.

That day in her office, and after a lot of back-and-forth, Jonelle made another promise. She said that for sure they would make the arrest over the summer, and wouldn't that be even better for Aaron? School isn't in session and it would be an easier time for him and his family to go into hiding for a while and less disruptive to his life and that of his siblings. She also pointed out that Penn State is not in session during the summer (except for a small group of summer students), so that would also take the heat off in terms of publicity.

When I picture what that summer looked like, I see an open calendar with the pages turning in the wind one by one. June, July, and then August comes . . . Even though I had been calling Jonelle all summer after that newest promise of an arrest, once again she didn't take my calls.

It's in my notes that on August 12, 2010, I had a session with Aaron, who was really getting depressed. It wasn't just anxiety that tormented him now, but true reactive depression because nothing was happening in the case. Aaron was now suffering from panic attacks as well as conversion disorder, a syndrome emanating from inordinate psychological stress, trauma, or conflict that presents with neurological symptoms. From a psychological point of view, the symptoms are thought to be the mind's attempt to resolve the conflict or trauma. Aaron was having such physical pains that he actually ended up in the hospital. He could barely breathe through the panic attacks. When they called me from the emergency room at Dawn's request, since Aaron's abdominal pain was excruciating and yet the doctors couldn't find anything medically wrong with him, I said to give him a little Ativan. I simply understood that his pain manifested itself physically but came from his mind. Ativan did the trick, but Ativan wasn't the answer. It was like putting a Band-Aid on something that required surgery. This case was dragging on and on with no end in sight. He was also starting to have suicidal ideation, because he felt that he couldn't take the stress anymore. He was so disillusioned that I feared he was truly beginning to come apart. I was sick of all the false promises, too, but my job was to keep Aaron's head above water.

I called Jonelle after that session on August 12 with Aaron, hoping to stress the urgency of the situation not only from the point of view of justice but with regard to Aaron's state of mind. After the first message, I heard nothing back. Finally, after I left several messages that were downright nasty, she called and said again that her hands remained tied. I said that Aaron was having panic attacks and suffering from conversion disorder, and actually ending up in the hospital because he was in such physical pain. Eventually I said that if we didn't have an answer about an arrest, we would be going to the FBI. Sandusky had transported a child over state lines when he took Aaron to Maryland. That meant this case was appropriate for the bureau. Jonelle asked me to give her twenty-four hours to get back to me. She called the next day but nothing had changed. They had no arrest date. It was still up to Corbett.

Because I was subpoenaed to the grand jury and under the legal restrictions by which neither Aaron nor I could talk about the case, I could not be the one to call the FBI. As for Aaron, even if he wasn't under subpoena, asking him to call the FBI was out of the question. The only one who could call was Dawn, since she wasn't under subpoena. My guess is that Jonelle thought we were just bluffing when it came to calling the FBI, and she even reminded me that I wasn't permitted to do so under the grand jury's restrictions. But she underestimated Dawn, who called the FBI office in Philadelphia. Dawn and I went over the script of sorts; she was to give the name of the victim and the name of the perpetrator. Even though she was understandably nervous, she told the story to an FBI agent and went as far as to say that she was convinced that the attorney general was dragging his feet because he happened to be running for governor. They listened, but at the end of the call they said they couldn't be of any assistance. As long as this was an open case and investigation, they couldn't intervene. They said if the case ended up closed without an arrest, we should call them back.

Believe it when I say I tried with all my might not to entertain a conspiracy theory, but the problem was that it was staring me right in the face. Even the FBI was powerless to intercede. I did more digging. Reports said that Corbett had accepted $640,000 in campaign donations from trustees of the Second Mile.

Now it was September 2010. The summer had come and gone, with promises of an arrest broken over and over again. Aaron was back in school. In the meantime, behind the scenes, an eager cub reporter named Sara Ganim, who worked the crime beat for a local paper in State College, had somehow gotten wind of the fact that a young boy had made some serious sexual allegations against Jerry Sandusky. A Penn State graduate and a Penn State football fan, Ganim knew exactly who Sandusky was and she also knew her way around the message boards at the university. Little did we all know at the time that there were rumors floating around those message boards and people were even posting blogs, and then others were commenting on the blogs. Most of the comments were from people who didn't believe for one second that Sandusky was guilty. Ultimately this would be a breaking story but right now it still remained dormant, merely steeped in rumor. Later we learned that Ganim even contacted Graham Spanier, the president of Penn State, to ask if he had any knowledge of an investigation of Sandusky for criminal activity while he was a Penn State employee. There was a definite leak somewhere.

One good thing happened in September 2010: Jerry Sandusky officially retired from the Second Mile, giving the explanation that he wanted to spend more time with his family and tend to personal matters. His statement made the news, but it wasn't earth-shattering—except to those of us who knew the real reason why.

Aaron's depression, anxiety, anger, and post-traumatic stress were coming to a boiling point. He was not a happy guy. And then in late October, he drove his car straight into a tree.

21

Hitting a Tree

Aaron

MY CAR ACCIDENT HAPPENED ON OCTOBER 21, 2010. I WAS SIX-
teen and in my sophomore year of high school. I had my license
now, so there were no more school buses for me and it was pretty
cool to be driving. That morning, Mom said that I really ought
to check the air in one of my tires. She said it looked low, but I
was running kind of late and had to pick up two of my friends. I
picked up the first guy and even though there was an air pump at
his house, and I thought about checking the tire, I still had to
pick up another friend. I just let it go. I didn't want to be late for
school. The three of us were finally on our way and I decided to
take all the back roads so I could avoid all the stoplights. I often
took the back roads because they lead you right to the main road
that goes into the school.

I don't remember too much from that morning. I just remember that as I went around the turn, I heard a loud boom and the
car whipped back and forth; I put both my hands on the steering
wheel and tried to control the car that was spinning like crazy. I
went to hit the brake, and I guess that I must have hit the accel-
erator by accident. That's when I stop remembering. I went about

sixty miles per hour into a tree. No one ever did find out whether it was a blowout that started the whole thing. I know that the car was just wrapped around that tree in a V. There were no airbags. It was an old car. My one friend in the front broke his foot and my other friend, who was sitting in the middle of the bench seat in the back, flew up and hit the dashboard. I know it was the dashboard because he had a big mark shaped like a dashboard around his head.

My friend with the head injury and I were airlifted to Geisinger Medical Center in Danville, where they have a big trauma unit. My other friend was taken to Lock Haven. I broke my hip and had a skull fracture and my face was all messed up. We weren't wearing seat belts, either. I never felt safe wearing a seat belt. After the accident, EMS said that if I had been wearing a seat belt, I probably would have died because of the way it would have jerked me. They said it would have caved in my ribs. My body hit the roof of the car, the windshield, and the steering wheel. There were a series of hairpin turns on that road—to the right and then to the left and then a straightaway and then another left. And then I lost control of the car.

As scary as the accident was, it was even scarier when the state police wanted to check out my car because they were worried about tampering. They were trying to determine how an Oldsmobile station wagon with more than three hundred thousand miles on it, which barely makes it up any hill even without the extra weight of two passengers, could accelerate so suddenly. They said it just didn't make sense. It didn't make sense to me, either, since usually when I tried to go up a hill, the car stalled out. I think I just lost control. There were wet leaves on the road and I think that it was just an accident. But it still bugged me that the car went sixty miles per hour right up an embankment. The state police were worried that either the car was purposely compromised or that there was another car that drove me off that road. I couldn't remember anything and neither could my friends. Mom and Mike were pretty concerned, though. In my gut, I just thought I'd wrecked my car. I was in the hospital for over a week.

Before the accident, I'd been doing a lot of running and not just for school. Running helped me to deal with all the stress and anger and depression. After the accident and after I got out of the hospital, I was so limited, and then I got even more frustrated and upset. They had me in a wheelchair and I couldn't stand it. I was a star distance runner and I thought there was no way that I should be confined in a wheelchair. So I tried walking around a little. But it really hurt, so then I'd take the wheelchair with me when I went out. I'd walk for a while and then use the chair if I had to, but I really tried to walk through the pain. It got to the point where I couldn't take being confined like that anymore. I needed to get out and do something physical.

Once I was able to walk, and even though it hurt because I was so banged up and broken, I started to run, despite what the doctors told me. My distance coach always told me that you had to run through pain and I was real good at that. Of course, he was probably talking about leg cramps or a stitch in your ribs and not the kind of pain that comes from a car accident. But I just kept running until I couldn't go anymore, and then I'd call a friend and someone would come and pick me up. I didn't follow anyone's directions or restrictions. Once the doctor said I could run again, not knowing that I had been doing that already, I really pulled out the stops and ran the way I always had. It did me a world of good.

But after the car accident and even after I started running, I started having nightmares again. This time they were all about the car accident. In all the dreams, there was Jerry and he was running my car off the road.

———————

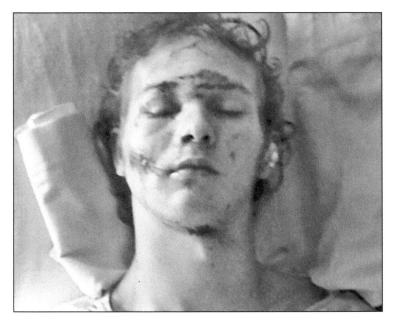

Aaron after the car accident

Dawn

THE STATE POLICE WERE FULLY AWARE OF AARON'S ACCIDENT. NOT only did they make sure it was truly an accident, but also, once they were assured that it was, they set up a whole security team at Geisinger. Aaron was even given a secret code name. We didn't want anyone snooping around and I sure didn't want him harmed. I also wasn't convinced that it was an accident at all. That car didn't have that kind of power.

Aaron hardly recalls anything after his car plowed into that tree. For one thing, he had a head injury. For another, the medical team put him in a drug-induced coma for the first few days. Until the doctors got back the results from all the tests and scans, they were concerned that there could be possible brain damage. There wasn't, but it was a serious concern. I know they erred on the side of caution, but I can't even begin to explain how I felt for those first few days as he just lay there.

After the coma was lifted, Aaron drifted in and out of consciousness. There were several times he appeared to stop breathing. One time, a nurse gave him CPR as I was yelling his name and he responded and started breathing again. Logically, I know it was more the CPR that revived him, but a part of me thinks that it was really my voice that got him going again. With a child, there's something about hearing a mother's voice, and mine was so desperate as I called for him to breathe.

It was touch-and-go for those eight days that he was in the hospital, and I was absolutely terrified. I was there every day. I never left his side. I sent Katie and Bubby to my parents as soon as I heard about the accident, and that's where they stayed until Aaron came home.

Aaron was in the Pediatric Intensive Care Unit, in a private room. There was a bench with a hard leather back that was built into the wall, with a little nightstand that cornered around. The staff gave me a pillow and a blanket and I slept on that bench every night with my feet resting on the wooden stand. Really, I hardly slept at all. I'd just close my eyes and then wake up with a start and check on Aaron to make sure he was breathing.

The nurses brought me hospital food, and sometimes my parents or friends would bring something in for me when they came to visit. If I needed to step outside for a smoke, I always made sure that a nurse was in the room with Aaron while I was gone. It wasn't until the last couple of days, when I knew he was out of the woods, that it was okay for me to leave. It was really because he wanted a chocolate milk shake, so I drove over to Wendy's.

I was extremely anxious and frightened, not only because of the severity of Aaron's injuries, but also because I couldn't stop wondering if this was really an accident or if someone had deliberately sabotaged his car. I feared for Aaron and my other children. I was in constant touch with Trooper Rossman, Tony Sassano, and Mike Gillum. I just needed to make sure that there was nothing new that I had to be aware of for both Aaron's sake and the rest of my family.

When Aaron came home, I was of course relieved but I didn't want him out of my sight. All of Aaron's fears about Sandusky were now more believable to me than ever before.

22

The Boy in the Shower

Mike

AARON HAD A ROUGH TIME AFTER THE ACCIDENT, BUT TO HIS credit, he recovered relatively quickly. Never mind that this kid was an athlete and a runner and suddenly he had to rely on a wheelchair and stay put; as he recovered he still had to look at an empty horizon in terms of Sandusky's arrest. He was getting angrier by the day at the attorney general's office, and I couldn't blame him—or dissuade him. All of us—Aaron, Dawn, and I— just felt we were being placated and strung along. We figured we'd just be drop-kicked at the end of it all and that would be it.

After Aaron's accident, I was trying to keep him in a news blackout. I didn't want him reading those stories that were popping up in the local paper and really stirring up the Internet. There was also new talk about the Ray Gricar case. All kinds of stories were circulating on blogs about Ray Gricar, and speculation about his ties to the mob and his relationship to Sandusky. My earlier suspicions that Sandusky's abuse went even deeper now seemed plausible.

It was no wonder that the state police didn't take Aaron's car accident lightly. Even after they vetted the Oldsmobile, I had a feeling they remained concerned that Aaron could be in some kind of danger. When Aaron was in the hospital, phone operators reported to Aaron's security team that a man identifying himself as "Matthew" called at least twenty times trying to locate Aaron by name. At one point, the man entered the hospital and made it to the third floor, where he asked for Aaron but was simply asked to leave. Hospital security did not detain him or ask for ID. We never did find out who he was. I figured he was probably a reporter, or was working with one, since the Internet was posting all the stuff about Sandusky and abuse, and that Aaron's name must have been leaked—but by whom? If the reporter was Ganim, who was her source and where was the leak?

Aaron eventually found out about the Ray Gricar story after his accident, and the story really flipped him out. You see, the story that I had read about Gricar a few months before had evolved. Now the blogs and message boards were saying that Gricar had been investigating a child sexual abuse case, and even though Gricar's case wasn't tied to Sandusky, Gricar's disappearance in 2005, coupled with the allegations against Sandusky, was becoming fodder for sensationalism.

The rumor mills and blogs were endless and Dawn became obsessed with them. She was on the computer 24/7, downloading these blog items and giving them to me. Dawn was searching for witnesses and victims, but she also wanted to make sure that Aaron's name didn't show up. I forwarded dozens upon dozens of them to Jonelle, as well as to Tony Sassano, who was now a key player. I didn't just send the blogs; I also sent the comments, which were far more revealing. Most of the comments defended Sandusky as the iconic figure that he was, but then there were plenty of anonymous comments from people who were saying that they knew for a fact that Jerry Sandusky was a pedophile.

There was one comment to a blog that I remember well, and which really hit me later on, once we were in trial. It was from an anonymous Penn State employee who had witnessed Sandusky engaging in anal sex with a little boy.

It was one thing to read the blogs and comments, but then I started getting phone calls from people as far away as Florida saying that Jerry Sandusky had abused them when they were kids. I asked why they were calling me and how they got my name in the first place. Someone on the Internet had pointed to CYS's involvement, and as the sole psychologist, it was easy to find my name and number.

The blogs were hitting too close to home now. Not only was it evident that other victims were out there; we were concerned that it was just a matter of time before Aaron's identity would be revealed. We worried that Aaron, as the first victim to come forward, the one who inspired others to purge secrets they'd hidden for years, could be a target of those who supported Sandusky. CYS was convinced that we had to move Dawn and her children so they would be protected.

It was early November 2010, and before we had a plan in place to move Dawn and the kids, the holidays came again, and we just hadn't gotten the plan off the ground yet.

There was still no talk of an arrest but those blogs and websites had altered the landscape. It was nearing the end of 2010 and Jonelle called to say that they had a witness who was a Penn State employee and was willing to testify that he witnessed a naked Jerry Sandusky in the locker room in a sexual position with a boy who looked to be around ten years old. The witness turned out to be Penn State assistant football coach Mike Mc-Queary. The attorney general's office intervened, and within twenty-four hours of our hearing the news that there was a second victim, many of the unauthorized blogs coming out of Penn State's student, alumni, faculty, and fan-based populations were taken down by the attorney general's office. The boy whom McQueary had seen would become known as Victim 2: the boy in the shower.

In February 2011, Sara Ganim knocked on Dawn's door. She asked if Dawn's son Aaron—shockingly using his name—was the boy who started the allegations against Sandusky. Dawn said she didn't know what the reporter was talking about. Ganim was determined and didn't stop there. She asked if Aaron ran on the school track team. Evidently Ganim had some solid sources. Dawn just turned her away and shut the door, then called me. Ganim must have somehow gotten her hands on the police report with all of our names on it. The fact that she found Dawn's address and knew Aaron's name was a major leak from the top. This was not just a blogger's guess. Ganim told Dawn she was going to run a story with or without Dawn's cooperation.

February might well be the cruelest month. It was for me. On February 22, 2011, while all this was happening in my world with Aaron, my brother Harold died of pancreatic cancer. Harold had told me his diagnosis just months before and I'd made a quick trip to visit him in California, but I had no idea his death would come so quickly.

I went to Harold's funeral and came back with a very heavy heart. But as it turned out, I barely had time to mourn.

23

Round Three

Mike

I HARDLY THOUGHT IT WAS A COINCIDENCE THAT AFTER ELECTION Day, November 2, 2010, when Tom Corbett won his campaign for governor of Pennsylvania, we suddenly heard that witnesses were coming forward. There was also a whole new flurry of activity and a lot of noise when it came to Sandusky and this case that had been bandied about for years. Corbett was securely in office and there was a new attorney general, Linda Kelly.

Finally, sometime in March 2011, four arduous months after the fall, when the blogs began to appear and witnesses and victims of Sandusky's crimes came forward, Jonelle called to say that there would be another grand jury on April 11, 2011. Think about it: Aaron first appeared in my office in November 2008. Not only was there another grand jury, but now the jurors were different. The terms of the last thirty jurors expired and this was a brand-new group of people who wanted to hear testimony. Aaron had to take it from the top again.

When Aaron heard that he had to testify in front of an entirely new grand jury, he hit a real low. The kid had had a horrible year—cruelly rejected by girlfriends, waiting for an arrest that seemed like it would never come, suffering through a terrible car accident. He was extremely anxious and there was no consoling him when it came to any belief in the justice system. He felt betrayed, completely let down, all but abandoned.

About a month before the grand jury convened, Trooper Rossman came in for a meeting with Aaron. I was of course present. Rossman wanted to know if Aaron was ever molested in the shower with Sandusky. Aaron responded strongly and said that he did not take showers with Sandusky. Rossman insisted that they had a report that a witness saw a boy who looked to be around Aaron's age with blond hair and a slim build just like Aaron. He said that the witness saw Sandusky molesting the boy in the athletic building's shower.

"We're not clear on the exact year," Rossman said. "Are you sure that boy wasn't you? We need to know whether we have another victim out there or not."

Aaron said over and over that it wasn't him. For days after that, Rossman and I were on the phone trying to pin down a timeline. When we finally realized that the witness, McQueary, saw the incident in March 2001, we did the math and realized that for sure we had another victim. This made Aaron feel better because there was a witness who was a credible adult. He felt better, vindicated in some ways, but still he was worn down and disillusioned. Vindicated is different from relieved. He was still unconvinced that the other witness and the other victim would make a difference. He was out of hope when it came to an arrest.

On March 31, 2011, one month after Ganim's surprise visit to Dawn and less than two weeks before the third grand jury, *The Patriot News* ran a front-page article by Sara Ganim: "Sandusky Faces Grand Jury Probe." Ganim kept her promise to Dawn that her story would run regardless of Dawn's cooperation. In the first paragraph, Ganim said that Sandusky was the subject of an investigation resulting from allegations that he indecently assaulted a teenage boy. Later in the piece, she identified the boy as a resident of Clinton County. Further down, after much background about Penn State officials and a history of the illustrious Jerry Sandusky as someone once considered Paterno's likely successor, she quoted John DiNunzio, the interim superintendent of the school district at the time of her story. Based upon DiNunzio's information, Ganim patched together an accounting of a mother and child making a report to the Bellefonte Area School District. The facts were vague and erroneous when it came to the mother and child account. Although she had already been to Dawn's house and had Aaron's name, she had the decency not to release it in the article. Or perhaps it wasn't released because laws are in place to protect the identity of a minor. Ganim, however, was dogged and we knew it. The headline piece was unsettling. Besides, this was becoming a game of who do you trust—and at that point, trust was a pretty tough call.

We were all worried that the press would be waiting for us when we got to the secret grand jury on April 11. Just like the last two times, we stayed overnight in Harrisburg the night before, but unlike the last two times, when secrecy was ensured, we were concerned that reporters would be waiting for us. The attorney general's office is in an area of Harrisburg called Strawberry Square, right across the street from the capitol building. There are shops and restaurants, and even though the attorney general's office is in a nondescript building, it's almost *too* nondescript as it stands there with no name. It simply doesn't fit in with the rest of the area and sticks out like a sore thumb. There were lots of people milling about, and although we didn't see anyone obvious—no one with a camera or tape recorder or a notebook— we wondered if any of the people were reporters incognito. Because there were leaks and the press was sniffing around, this time we were picked up at our motel in a van with blacked-out windows and we entered the building through an underground garage. Agents took us through a secret entrance and we were whisked into the grand jury room. It was like something out of a movie.

As Dawn, Aaron, and I were escorted to the waiting area, I caught a glimpse of an adult male who was waiting in a pre-testimony room. Jonelle and Tony had verified prior to this that they had another victim who was now an adult and was there to testify. I wondered if the door to the room where he waited had been intentionally or accidentally left open. Typically, the witnesses are sequestered behind a closed door. Aaron saw the young man as well. He was in his mid-twenties, fidgety, and then he looked up and made eye contact with us. Even if I hadn't been told that there would be another of Sandusky's victims at the grand jury, I would have known by the look in that young man's hollow eyes that he was a victim. He also had a similar physical presentation to Aaron, if Aaron were ten years older. It hit me hard how long this had been going on with Sandusky. I figured for a good fifteen years—if not more.

Aaron

THIS NEW GRAND JURY ALLOWED ME TO READ MY TESTIMONY, SINCE I had given it twice before. I thought that might make it easier, but as it turned out, it was worse to read my own words out loud. I almost felt like it would have been better if I'd been cross-examined. They gave me shorter pauses in between my readings than in the previous times, when I was on the stand for a long time and then they gave me a longer break. I was so nervous. I could have taken some meds to calm myself down, but Mike said that I really needed to be alert. But as I read my own words, it made me feel as though someone was beating me up. It was like living through everything Jerry had done to me. I couldn't stop crying when I was reading, and when it was finally over and I walked out of that courtroom, I literally cried on my mom's shoulder. It was like I was that little kid again who wanted someone to know what was happening and save me, but this time I could tell the truth.

Other than what happened to me with Jerry, those three grand juries were the worst experiences of my life. Each time, I could barely get through them and wasn't sure that I would. It was no surprise that after the third one, the nightmares started picking up speed again, but this time I was also sleepwalking. Mom would catch me walking around the apartment in the middle of the night, and when she came up to me, she said I would just start yelling and screaming stuff like "get away" and "leave me alone," like someone was trying to hurt me. Even when I was asleep, I never rested. I still felt threatened.

All little kids go through this time when they think there are monsters out to get them and then if you're lucky, your mom leaves a light on and she checks behind the curtains and under the bed and you figure if the monsters were there, they're gone now. My monster was real, and even after that third grand jury I had my doubts about people believing me. I figured that the other guy who was there that day was also one of Sandusky's victims and I wondered whether the grand jury would believe him, either.

24

Going the Distance

Mike

AFTER THE THIRD GRAND JURY, TROOPER ROSSMAN WAS GONE. Jonelle said that Rossman was simply no longer on the case because her new boss, Linda Kelly, had decided to form a brand-new task force which consisted of six agents working with her from the attorney general's office as well as law enforcement from the state police.

My first reaction was that they should have had that all along, and Jonelle said that it really wasn't until the last couple of months that the boss, Kelly, realized the enormity of the case. She started to tell me about yet another witness, someone other than McQueary, as well as a third victim, but she still wasn't naming anyone. Honestly, I had a million questions that I didn't ask, because I was fuming. I wanted to ask her why Corbett had dragged his feet but I knew the obvious answer. Now that Corbett was governor and there was no risk of antagonizing anyone who might have interfered with his election, there was a whole new mindset in the attorney general's office. Now Kelly was tackling the case, as opposed to Corbett, who had been willing to just let it roll.

Jonelle said that Kelly wanted to complete the investigation and really invest all the time and resources into the case that it deserved. And once again, Jonelle told me they were moving toward an arrest. Now it was the end of May 2011. Suffice it to say that there was a huge credibility gap between me and Jonelle at that point. I'd believe an arrest when it happened.

By three months later, come August 2011, I'd had it. I demanded to talk with Linda Kelly personally. We'd already called the FBI and knew they couldn't do a thing unless the case was closed without an arrest; there was no action that I could see. I just decided that I needed to go right to the top in order to get to the bottom of it all.

Jonelle said that a meeting with Kelly wasn't possible, but I could meet with her and Frank Fina, whose position in the hierarchy was somewhere in between Jonelle and Kelly. Jonelle referred to Fina as her boss, so I assumed he had some sort of seniority, although this was the first time I'd heard his name. We made arrangements for the meeting and the night before, near the end of August, I drove the three of us—Dawn, Aaron, and myself—to Harrisburg. In the morning, we were picked up in the van with the blacked-out windows and whisked secretly into Fina's office in the secret building in Strawberry Square. This time the media presence outside was obvious. So much for secrets. Reporters were hanging around ready to pounce, but agents got us into that underground garage and up to the offices without any problem.

The meeting lasted three hours and it wasn't just Jonelle and Fina. Tony Sassano was there as well. Since I'd requested the meeting, I assumed the lead without asking. I told them I was tired of all the false promises when it came to an arrest. I said that we had a depressed and anxious boy here who had been hospitalized three times for panic attacks and conversion syndrome. I said that we had a mother who feared for her entire family. I was really angry. I asked them to come clean and tell me precisely what gives, since I knew they had witnesses and other victims.

It was the same old song and dance in reply. "This is a big case and we could be severely scrutinized so we have to do things properly."

When I argued that they had had ample time to do things "properly" and now had witnesses and other victims, Fina threw the state police under the bus and said they didn't do the greatest investigation. Fina said they all had to go back and clean up some "stuff" before an arrest could be made.

I demanded an arrest date. Fina was getting steamed, too. He said he wasn't going to arrest Sandusky tomorrow and I said, I'm not saying to arrest him tomorrow, but it's got to happen soon and with an exact date. I went so far as to say that if they didn't give me a date and stick to it, we were just going to take the story to the media.

Now, we all knew that the media already had wind of what was happening, but I had the real facts. I wished I had a real plan, but I knew there were too many constraints on me. The grand jury was secret and if I said anything to the media about their proceedings, as someone who had been subpoenaed, I could get arrested. If I got arrested, I could lose my license. Damned if I was going to get arrested before Sandusky did, but I swear, at that point the possibility of my arrest was the only thing that stopped me from going to the media.

Dawn said that she could go to the media, and then I said that they were all just covering their butts again at Aaron's expense. *This kid is going to end up dying from all of this, so what's the point of your task force and investigation?*

That was when Aaron stood up. Until that moment, he was just sitting there, seemingly taking it all in. Now he looked them all in the eye and said, "I'm out."

They sang like a chorus: "What do you mean?"

"That's it," Aaron said. "I'm not going to be your witness anymore."

Fina was saying stuff like "You just wait a minute" and "Hang on there," but Aaron said he meant it. He'd had it at that point. If not for my pushing him along, he might have backed out a long time before this, and to this day I still question myself about how much I pushed him.

When Aaron said he was out, I wondered whether I was doing the right thing for him. We had come so far and things were breaking in the papers, and on one hand I wanted that bastard Sandusky in jail and for other children to be safe, but on the other hand, all we had were broken promises, and what would happen if Aaron refused to testify and cooperate?

In that moment, Aaron went from a frightened little boy to a young man with incredible courage.

Fina said they'd have Sandusky arrested by the end of the year, but he was pissed off. Not at Aaron or Dawn—he was pissed off at me because I still didn't believe him. I can't remember whether I said it out loud but for sure I thought, "Okay, twenty percent he'll keep his word, but eighty percent it's probably bullshit."

They took us back out through the basement labyrinth and the garage and to the waiting van with the blacked-out windows. They drove us to my car in the motel parking lot. But as we were leaving the building that day, this time I looked around at all the people in their cubicles and offices. For the first time, I was struck by all the Penn State souvenirs. There were emblems, banners, flags, and coffee mugs plastered with Nittany Lions. It was a sea of blue and white.

On the three-hour drive home, we didn't say much at all.

25

The Arrest

Aaron

IT WAS NOVEMBER 2011, THREE MONTHS AFTER OUR MEETING WITH the attorney general. I was certain that nothing would ever come of an arrest when it came to Jerry. Even though he had left the Second Mile, I figured he'd just lay low and everything would eventually die down. It didn't matter that there was another victim, or maybe two others or whatever it was they were telling me. It didn't matter that there were witnesses. It just seemed hopeless. It had been three long years since I first walked into Mike's office at Children and Youth in my hometown, where I thought nothing much ever happened.

Honestly, by November, I'd given up. Even though I tried to push all the thoughts away, they were always in the back of my mind and I thought about that day when I first met Jerry Sandusky and I was eleven years old. How different things could be if the school hadn't suggested I go to the camp at the Second Mile. It sounded like it would be a lot of fun and besides, when you're a kid and an adult like your mom or your teacher says that something will be good for you, you do it. I kept thinking how that week changed the rest of my life. What if I had just done what I did most summers and hung out with my friends? We

played catch and chase and flag football. We swam in the dam.
We rode our bikes around the neighborhood and hung out.
That's what you do when you're eleven and it was good enough
for me.

In some ways, it was just a regular Saturday morning. Let me
say it this way—it was as regular as Saturday mornings were for
the last six years of my life, since everything changed. It was as
regular as I tried to make any morning feel in the three years
since I walked into Mike's office and told him what had happened to me.

I'd had therapy with Mike on Thursday. On Friday night,
Mike called me with a heads-up that the attorney general's office
had called him and said the arrest of Jerry Sandusky was going
to happen over the weekend.

The truth is, we had been through this so many times before,
with the attorney general saying there would be an arrest. This
was the first time that Mike sounded real definite. He said it really was going to happen this time. I didn't buy it. I said, "Yeah,
right. We've heard this before."

I trusted Mike, but we had both been lied to so many times by
the lawyers who said that Jerry was about to be arrested. My
mind started racing ahead and I was thinking that I'd have to give
more grand jury testimony and do more interviews with the state
police until someone finally believed that what I was saying about
Jerry was true. I really didn't believe that Jerry would ever be arrested, because he was who he was. He just had all the power and
the right people behind him and we didn't. I felt like they were
just saying that it was about to finally happen and then they'd
find a way to get out of it again. I was frustrated and getting
angry all over again.

So, on that Saturday around noon, after another night when I
couldn't sleep and stayed up late because I thought if I did then
the nightmares wouldn't come soon, I was sitting in my living
room, watching TV and playing video games and trying to get

rid of all the thoughts in my head that were making me feel shaky. I was angry, but I felt sad, too.

For whatever reason, I didn't sleep late that morning even though I hadn't slept much the night before. My cellphone rang, and not too many people have my cell number. It was Tony Sassano, who said that Jerry Sandusky had been arrested. It felt like what I was hearing wasn't real. Just around the same time that my cell rang, Mike called my mom on her cell. He told me later that he called my mom because even though the news was real and exciting, he didn't want to wake me with news like that if I was sleeping. I spoke to Mike and then it was like everything started going crazy. Mom's cell was ringing about the arrest and then Mom got on the Internet and turned on the television and there was the news all over the place.

So, now it was done. Finally, the arrest was made. I was sitting there and even though a part of me started to feel excited and happy, I was really more scared, to the point that I thought, Okay, now he's been arrested, and if he goes to jail, someone is going to hurt me and my family. It was just weird. I never thought the arrest would happen, and when it did, something didn't feel right about it. I guess I felt that just because he was arrested, it didn't mean it was over. I also knew there were a lot of people out there who believed he shouldn't have been arrested in the first place.

I started thinking about the fact that there would be a trial and that meant more testimony from me and I didn't want to do that again. I knew I would have to but I didn't know how long it would take. I had already testified three times before the grand juries. A trial would mean testifying a fourth time. Mike told me there would also be a preliminary hearing and then there would be the trial. How much more could I tell my story to strangers and hope they believed me?

The arrest came right before my eighteenth birthday. They say that eighteen is the emancipation birthday but that never occurred to me at the time. When I turned eighteen, I wanted to be excited, but instead I kept thinking about all the stuff I was about to go through and I just wanted it all to be over. With everything that happened in the last six years right up to now, even with Jerry's arrest, I felt more like I was on a collision course. I had this awful feeling that just because he was arrested, it wasn't over. There were too many people out there who still believed that Jerry was innocent. Once he posted bail, I thought, *See, this is how they'll treat him and he's going to end up walking.*

Dawn

THE DAY OF THE ARREST IS SUCH A BLUR IN MY MIND. I THINK IT WAS Tony Sassano who texted me the news, and then I remember being on the phone with Mike. Most of all, I remember telling Aaron not to answer his cellphone if he got calls from numbers he didn't recognize. A couple of weeks later, I moved my family to a new apartment and got two big dogs, a Saint Bernard and a Lab, even though I already had two dogs. I figured that having dogs might keep out anyone who tried to get to us, and the more dogs the better. Honestly, all I remember thinking was that I was glad that Sandusky was in jail, but then he got out on bail and all the stuff with Penn State was happening on the news and it seemed like this was bigger than I ever dreamed it would be. I just wanted to protect my kids.

Mike

JONELLE CALLED ME ON FRIDAY AFTERNOON, NOVEMBER 4, 2011, and said that the attorney general's office filed charges to make an arrest of Jerry Sandusky the following week. I knew that once they filed, the petition would appear online, and I knew that newspaper reporters and all media monitor the Internet. I also knew that the press was keeping a close watch on this case, which was really starting to boil behind the scenes.

The reporters caught news of the petition, and even though Jonelle said they took down the information really fast, it was too late and it was out there. No one can keep up with the transmission of electronic information. After all these years, I'm thinking, You've got to be kidding me. We've waited and waited and now it's just so bungled and Jonelle said that because the media got wind of it all, they'd have to move up the arrest now. I guessed that Sandusky was a flight risk.

Understand that as thrilled as I was, Dawn and I had wanted some notice so we could get her and the kids to a safe place. We wanted time for them to pack, and to explain to Bubby and Katie what was going on and not just make them run out of the apartment with the clothes on their backs.

Once we heard that an arrest was impending, Dawn and I were communicating and trying to determine other measures to protect their identities from the press. Jonelle said that Aaron's name would never appear, but then she said that his initials would appear. It was ridiculous to think that reporters couldn't figure out who Aaron was from initials. Ganim already knew, and had been at their house back in February. Now there was backlash from Penn State people—students, faculty, and fans—and the vocal ones were on the side of Sandusky. We were scrambling. A few days later, Dawn would move to a different address with the kids and get a Saint Bernard and a Lab in addition to the two old dogs she had, but we didn't have a chance to get them anywhere safe before the arrest.

I was at home on Saturday morning, November 5, 2011, when I got the news from Jonelle that the arrest had been made.

The next thing we knew, Sandusky was released on bail the following day. Here you have this guy who was arrested on forty counts of child sexual abuse and he's immediately released on one hundred thousand dollars bail? When I first heard the news anchor mention the amount of bail, I thought he meant to say one *million* dollars bail. That bail was nothing for him, with his money and all his resources. It was like being released on five dollars. Sandusky was brought to the district magistrate's office in cuffs and released? Later, news reports revealed that the magistrate who decided the bail, Judge Leslie Dutchcot, was a volunteer at the Second Mile. I wondered if she should have recused herself.

Sandusky posted bail and went home under unsecured house arrest. I wondered if this guy could be charged with the rapes of all these little boys and walk. I knew of people in the system over the years who were arrested on far fewer counts and had either no bail or way higher bail than Sandusky's.

I was outraged. I thought, So this is the way that the judicial system works in Sandusky's home turf of Centre County. This is how they're going to handle this guy—with kid gloves. Sandusky was back in his Penn State backyard.

Within days, everything shifted. The breaking news story was no longer about the victims. It wasn't even so much about the alleged perpetrator Sandusky. There was an announcement that Penn State would be holding a press conference the next day, but it was canceled. A hush fell over the Happy Valley.

26

The Walls Come Down

Mike

THE BREAKING NEWS WASN'T ABOUT THE CRIMES COMMITTED BY Sandusky. It was all about Penn State, and above all, it was about the iconic Joe Paterno. I was reading the papers and watching the news and trying to keep up with everything just like the rest of the world was. I still have boxes filled with piles of news clips in my office.

In addition to the arrest of Sandusky based upon the grand jury's recommendation that they found evidence that he molested eight boys whom he met through the Second Mile, there were charges against Penn State athletic director Tim Curley and Gary Schultz, Penn State's interim senior vice president for finance and business. Schultz was also the one who oversaw the Penn State police. The grand jury found that Curley and Schultz had lied during their testimony with regard to information they had received about a report of sexual abuse involving Sandusky. The two were charged with perjury, which is a felony, and failing to report abuse. The attorney general's office went public now with hotlines set up at their offices and with the state police, asking anyone with information about other possible victims, and asking any other victims themselves, to come forward.

It was Mike McQueary's testimony at the grand jury that was possibly the most damning when it came to what was now being viewed as a massive cover-up at Penn State. McQueary, although not initially named in the press and merely referred to as a former graduate assistant, testified that he witnessed Sandusky assaulting a naked boy around ten years old in the shower in 2001. The grand jury called McQueary an "extremely credible witness."

Reports said that the witness testified that he had first spoken with his own father and then notified Paterno the next day. Paterno then reported the incident to Curley. In a meeting with Curley and Schultz about a week later, the witness was assured that they would investigate the incident. Paterno was not at the meeting. During the grand jury testimony, Curley called the activity in the shower between the child and Sandusky "horsing around" and also denied that McQueary said it was of a sexual nature. Schultz testified at the grand jury that the allegations proved not to be serious and there was no indication that a crime occurred. He also testified that he was aware that Sandusky had been investigated for similar allegations in 1998. University president Graham Spanier said he knew nothing of a 1998 investigation.

It wasn't a week after Sandusky's arrest that both Spanier and Paterno were fired. Although neither Paterno nor Spanier was charged in the case (unlike Curley and Schultz), there were far too many questions about the fact that Spanier and Paterno had knowledge of Sandusky's alleged sexual abuse and failed to act in a way that could have stopped him. Spanier was saying that Curley and Schultz would be proven innocent and I was wondering how he could possibly support these two guys who were covering it all up.

The campus seemed to go into a state of shock. Thousands of students lined the streets, blowing vuvuzelas and air horns, and pumping their fists in the air chanting, "We want Joe!" Cops in riot gear were sending out clouds of pepper spray and trying to hold them back as the students toppled a news van, knocked down street signs and trash cans, and set off firecrackers. It looked like a war zone. The students weren't rioting because there had been a seeming cover-up when it came to Sandusky and the sexual crimes he allegedly committed, but because "JoePa" was fired. Students rallied outside JoePa's home, calling out "We are Penn State!" A frail Paterno came to his doorstep and responded, "That's right. We are Penn State and don't ever forget it."

Students were supporting Paterno, not believing for a second that he had turned a blind eye to all of this. The attorney general's office told us that Paterno had fulfilled the chain of command and legally did what he was supposed to do by reporting the incident in the shower to his superiors. I kept thinking that yes, he reported the incident, but then no one took action against Sandusky. He still had his keys to the campus and he was able to run free. He was still bringing kids on campus, allowed to use that indoor pool at the hotel nearby, and he was still at the Second Mile. Maybe Paterno didn't break any laws, but morally he did nothing when he saw that Curley and Schultz did nothing. Paterno remained silent. It was my opinion that the attorney general's office was so afraid of backlash that they didn't say or do anything about Paterno. They weren't going to hold his feet to the fire. Really, they wanted to disassociate from Paterno and say nothing that was negative. The stakes were too high.

In some way, I had always looked up to Paterno, even though I wasn't a diehard football fan. I thought he was a wonderful man and coach who held high standards for his players. He didn't accept any bad behavior and made sure the players all maintained good grades. I met him once by accident, long before all this happened. We both happened to be at the Nittany Lion Inn on campus. I still have this classic box of Wheaties with Paterno on the cover of the box. Now all I could think was, How could he have done nothing? How could he not have sought justice regardless of who the perpetrator was? I was disillusioned. For me, Paterno was guilty by omission.

On Monday, November 7, 2011, Attorney General Linda Kelly held a press conference stating that Sandusky was arrested on forty counts of child sexual abuse. That was when the term "Victim 1" was first used. Kelly was flanked by Frank Fina, Jonelle Eshbach, and the commander of the Pennsylvania State Police. They had a chart behind them showing a timeline, and there was Victim 1 in a silhouette. Kelly stated that there were nine known victims as well as "the boy in the shower," who had yet to be identified because he had not come forward. Even that press conference went quickly from Sandusky's alleged sexual crimes against children to the press asking a million questions about Paterno. Kelly kept trying to dodge them, emphatically saying that Joe Paterno was not the subject of the investigation.

As I watched it all unfold within those two days after Sandusky's arrest, I was worried about Aaron's mental health being compromised, as much if not more so than I was worried that his name would be revealed. You couldn't avoid the news about this breaking case. There were even news tickers about it crawling across the bottom of the screen on the cable channels. Usually those crawlers are reserved for terrorist threats or maybe a tornado warning, but this case was dominating the news—nationally, not just locally. I was sitting there and thinking that Penn State is crumbling; that Aaron, Dawn, and I are responsible for bringing down an institution. I kept going over everything in my mind, and assuring myself that we did the right thing. But I was the one who pushed Dawn and Aaron and kept pressing forward. I exposed so many people who I didn't even know were part of a cover-up. It was what my instincts had been telling me all along. This case ran deep.

I thought back to Corbett and I was sure he didn't want to alienate Penn State and all of the fans as he ran for office. I thought about what I felt now for sure was his stalling. I wondered if it was all happening because Dawn contacted the FBI, I threatened to go to the media, and Aaron said he was out. We were all so tenacious. If we hadn't kept pushing, the attorney general's office might have dodged this whole thing and said that our witness wasn't strong enough.

It wasn't the Sandusky case that enraged people and the press. It wasn't the fact that little boys were lured and sexually assaulted by a man whose crimes were "more than probably" known to the higher-ups at Penn State. The press was far more concerned with Paterno. JoePa was fired; his more than illustrious career ended not only precipitously but ignominiously and unfairly. They wanted justice for JoePa. How could no one be concerned about justice when it came to the victims of Sandusky?

The press and all media were in full swing, and suddenly countless media showed up at my private office—not the one at CYS. I don't know how they found me but they arrived in droves. Networks, cable news, ESPN, and print media. They waited for me outside in the street and some even camped out in my waiting room. I didn't avoid them. I simply told them that I wasn't at liberty to discuss the case.

All hell was breaking loose at Penn State, and then it literally hit too close to home when the press showed up at my house. My wife and kids were frightened—not so much by the reporters at our home but by the knowledge that Sandusky supporters were out there along with people who were angry that Paterno was a casualty of all this. I couldn't discuss the case with anyone until the arrest was made—as I said before, not even my wife knew anything other than I had a big case and it involved abuse by a celebrity perpetrator. Now that the news broke, and as this domino effect was happening at Penn State, its administration unraveling, my wife and kids knew that I was in the thick of it.

Then things really started to get out of hand. The press was one thing, but when people who were just Penn State fans started to call me and make threats, I got worried. It was so bad that even my *ex*-wife was concerned about me. It got personal, too. Everyone I knew—family, friends, colleagues, neighbors—was a huge Penn State fan. I had always considered myself casually included among them; now I felt like an outsider.

A lot of my friends and family didn't believe that something like this could be true about either Sandusky or, to a greater extent, Paterno and Penn State. Friends and family were trying to be supportive of me, but mostly they were just in disbelief and mourning the accusations against Penn State. Even my colleagues were angry with me. They were polite but offered little support and wanted little if any dialogue with me. Core people supported me in the psychological organization in Pennsylvania and the people at CYS were there for me, but there were too many other colleagues who stayed neutral or stayed away. There was an ominous silence. How could people lose sight of what happened to these kids? Paterno was a legend and I never before realized how intensely people lived and breathed Penn State and football.

While all this was happening, the circumstances around Gricar's disappearance were revealed in the media and spawned questions about Jerry Sandusky. Anthony De Boef, who had worked with Gricar for five years as an assistant district attorney, said that although Gricar didn't share any information with him, Gricar was investigating a 1998 child sexual abuse case. Gricar was meticulous and had a reputation for not pandering to those in positions of political, social, or academic power. Presumably, Gricar had notes and/or recordings of two conversations between Sandusky and the victim's mother. The boy told his mother that Sandusky had showered with him naked. When the mother confronted Sandusky, he begged for forgiveness. What Sandusky didn't know was that Gricar had set up a sting in the eleven-year-old's house as Sandusky confessed and asked for absolution. Sounded to me like Gricar had him. Ultimately, Gricar dropped the case.

When I first read the story about Gricar that night after the first grand jury, there was no connection to Sandusky. He was just a guy like me who liked to drive, to go antiquing, and was described as a prosecutor who refused to bow to anyone. Now, as I learned more about Gricar and his connections to Sandusky, and then as the media somehow found my home and private office after Sandusky's arrest, I was concerned. Not to mention that a friend of mine called to warn me about a conversation he overheard when he was on the Penn State campus. A group of businessmen, clearly stating my name, said there were people who wanted me dead. I never hunted, but I always liked target shooting, so I can aim. I got a carry permit and bought a handgun. One night I was leaving my office and headed to my car. It was the only one left in the lot. This scraggy-looking guy appeared out of nowhere from a dark corner and came up to me. I drew my gun and he ran. I still don't know who he was. Maybe he was just drunk or stoned, but I felt threatened. When I pulled out the gun, he went the other way fast. It's a burden to carry a firearm. You have to think carefully and twice when you draw. The problem was that after Sandusky's arrest, I felt like the target.

Aaron

WHEN THE NEWS STARTED BREAKING AFTER JERRY WAS ARRESTED, I withdrew from a lot of people. It was hard being around the kids at school who were talking about what was going on. A lot of them said that someone was just making up stories because they wanted money. I tried to act real casual and say, "Yeah, right," like I wasn't the outsider that I felt I was. Somehow I'd just sneak away and let them go on talking.

There was a story in *The New York Times* that gave everything but my name. The reporter said that the kid who was now called Victim 1 ran on the track team at Central Mountain High and lived in a public housing complex in Lock Haven. It also said the kid had no father, had two siblings, and had gone to the Second Mile. The reporter even spoke to one of our neighbors, who said I was wearing fancy designer clothes at one point, and then he said that one day he heard me screaming that I didn't want to go with Jerry. None of that was true, and when the guy mentioned my school and the track team, kids started giving me a real hard time. Even though I said it wasn't me, they knew, and I was afraid of some of them because they were threatening to beat me up.

The track team stuck by me, though. I did have friends that I could have confided in on the team, but I didn't like talking about it to people. The guys and girls on my distance team, they all knew. They figured it out but also there came a point when I was giving some clues. It was getting tough to hold it inside. They knew but they didn't tell a soul and were loyal to me. They asked if I wanted to talk and said they'd listen to me any time. When I said that I didn't want to, they let it be and respected my wishes.

In January, I changed schools. Mom got me into a charter school that was farther away and we made a deal with them that any student who harassed me would be expelled; also, I could still run track for Central Mountain High.

I didn't want to be known as a victim, because I wasn't one anymore.

27

Enter Joe McGettigan

Mike

It was hard to believe that it had been three years since that scared boy from Central Mountain High walked into my office. On one hand, it seemed like yesterday, and on the other, it seemed like forever. Although I always felt there were others abused by Sandusky, I never imagined the magnitude of this. In my wildest dreams, I never thought this would evolve into the biggest scandal in the history of sports. All I knew was that Aaron wasn't the only one.

Shortly after the arrest, there was a shakeup behind the scenes when Kelly pulled Jonelle off as lead prosecutor and put in a guy named Joe McGettigan. I had put it out there to Kelly that Aaron thought being questioned by a man was more comfortable, and my guess was that the other victims might feel the same way. When Jonelle questioned Aaron during the grand jury proceedings, things didn't go especially well. I'm not sure of all Kelly's reasons behind the change but I gave her my input before it happened.

In early December 2011, Sandusky faced additional charges. Although his arrest the month before was based upon forty counts of sexual abuse, brought forth by eight accusers, two more victims had come forward. The latest victims testified before a grand jury that they had been raped and molested by Sandusky.

Sandusky was taken from his home to the Bellefonte Courthouse and bail was now set at $250,000. Prosecutors asked for $1 million bail. Even though the attorney general's office didn't get the higher bail, the terms differed now. The last bail was unsecured, but this time even if Sandusky was able to post bail, he would be subject to house arrest and would have to wear an electronic ankle monitor. It was also stated that he could have no contact with witnesses, his accusers—or any minors. Sandusky was now *definitely* viewed as a flight risk.

Sandusky made bail the following day. According to the press, he gathered the bail money by using $200,000 in real estate holdings and a certified check for $50,000 from Dottie. The blogs were changing. People were wondering if Sandusky was getting financial assistance from some "higher-ups," and people were questioning the depths of Sandusky's pockets. Although they maintained their loyalty to JoePa, they were coming to realize that the ten victims who came forward had strength in truth and numbers. There weren't many who questioned whether Sandusky was a true serial pedophile. But there were still thousands who felt that Paterno was beloved and wronged.

Sandusky's preliminary hearing was on December 13. A judge was brought in from western Pennsylvania to ensure objectivity, even though the trial venue remained in the town of Bellefonte, in Centre County. The town closed off the downtown square where the old stone courthouse stood. Armed police lined the streets and took positions on rooftops. The media presence was enormous, with hundreds of cars and vans and reporters.

I'd prepared Aaron for the preliminary hearing, knowing that it wouldn't be too much different from the trial itself. Aaron was totally psyched and ready to go, even though he was still upset when he thought that he'd have to tell his story once again, and then yet again at the trial. There was a big buildup for this hearing and then boom!

Joe McGettigan said, "Yes, my victims are here and they're ready to testify, Your Honor."

Amendola approached the bench and said, "We're going to waive the hearing."

It was all a game. For sure, the renunciation of the hearing was strategic. Amendola was probably banking that the victims were too shaken up and anxious to testify against Sandusky. The big question in everyone's mind was whether or not Aaron was going to show up and testify, and now there was also Witness 2, who had suffered substantial abuse over a long period of time. These boys were the two main witnesses against Sandusky, and Sandusky and Amendola were expecting that these kids wouldn't be able to hold up and would just crumble. When they heard that the witnesses were there and ready to go, Amendola waived the hearing. In addition, the prosecution had testimony from the mother of yet a third victim stating that Sandusky had pleaded with her son not to testify. This was not the boy from the infamous shower scene, whose identity was unknown at the time, but yet another boy who claimed to have been raped in the shower by Sandusky. Amendola saw that the cards were stacked against them.

There was talk that maybe Amendola and the attorney general were working on a plea deal behind the scenes. It was also conjectured that they waived the hearing because it was a way for Sandusky to see his accusers and then for Amendola to build his defense. Sandusky still maintained that all the boys, now men, were liars. Aaron, like the other victims, felt that this was just Sandusky screwing with them again. Really, the young men were the ones who stood up to Sandusky. It was a challenge to get Aaron to realize that at the time.

When Sandusky left the courthouse that day with his wife and a few of his kids, he addressed the press and restated his innocence. Using a football metaphor he said, "We're going to stay the course and fight this for all four quarters." Amendola addressed the press and contended that the alleged victims were frauds and just out for money.

Sandusky also waived an arraignment scheduled for January and another preliminary hearing in May 2012. Again it was a question of time just dragging on and on. Except for the fact that Sandusky was arrested and removed from the population, things were still not moving fast enough for me or Dawn and Aaron. The delay was a silver lining, though, since Aaron got to know McGettigan—and McGettigan got to know him and the other victims as well.

Aaron and I met again with McGettigan at the attorney general's secret office in Centre County, which now felt even closer to the Penn State campus in State College. It was quite a scene in that unassuming building. There's a drug task force housed in there, so the place is filled with undercover police and undercover narcotics detectives who look all scruffy, but they're cops. It was like another scene out of a movie.

Joe McGettigan is quite a character. He could have starred in *Men in Black*. He's got smooth white hair and wears signature black sunglasses. When he's not in court, he wears jeans, a pink polo shirt, and sneakers. He's sixty-two, six feet tall, extremely fit—and he smokes. He's the picture of the top gun, and he is one. He's the one who prosecutes multiple murders and awful abuse cases. He was even a volunteer over in Iraq, helping them to establish a justice system. That's the kind of guy Joe is. He used to be a district attorney in Philadelphia. When you get right down to it, he's tough as nails when it comes to getting justice, but he's also just a regular guy and so humane.

When Aaron first met Joe, he was somewhat intimidated, but then Joe put him at ease. It wasn't so much that Joe intimidated Aaron; it was that he was yet another new guy on the case. After Rossman faded from the picture, there was another trooper named Liter who stepped in briefly. Tony Sassano often accompanied Liter when they would show Aaron a picture of a boy to see if Aaron could make an identification. There were a couple of boys whom Aaron recognized—one kid who hung out with Sandusky and another whom Aaron knew from the Second Mile. The one from the Second Mile was with Sandusky and Aaron at a hotel swimming pool near State College.

It didn't take long for Joe to put Aaron at ease. He was personable, kind, and gracious. One time, he did get on Aaron's case because he was chewing tobacco. At the time, Joe was smoking a cigarette but he said that Aaron was young and an athlete and he should quit now.

When Joe was first getting to know Aaron, he tried to get him to respond to his questions without being intrusive. He kept apologizing and starting every session we had by saying, "I wish I didn't have to ask you this but . . ." Then he'd read back Aaron's grand jury testimony and say, "These are absolutely your words, right?" Joe didn't want any inconsistencies or slip-ups. He told Aaron that he wanted Aaron to be 100 percent comfortable with his testimony, and that was when Aaron visibly relaxed. There was a trust between the two of them that was crucial.

Aaron wasn't the only boy Joe talked with during the pretrial period. He interviewed and met with all the other victims as well. One time when Joe and I were alone together, just standing out in the parking lot and talking, Joe confessed that this Sandusky case made him sick. He said that there was one victim who was particularly troubled and Joe wanted to bounce some things off me and make sure that he was handling him correctly from a psychological point of view, since I had been counseling Aaron for so many years now. He also wanted to know a little more about Aaron and I gave him an overview. One day, after hours of talking about the profiles of the victims, we took a walk. I'll never forget what Joe said that day.

"Jerry Sandusky is one sick son of a bitch."

He went on to say that based upon the visuals of all the victims, Sandusky had a definite type. Joe called them "all those poor little kids" and remarked how their photographs from younger days showed that they were all slight, and many of them were blond and delicate boys—not only in stature but because they were from homes that were broken as well.

Joe was fearless when it came to prosecuting the case, but when it came to the boys themselves, he was worried about them on a human level. As a group, none of them had told anyone before what happened to them with Sandusky. They'd kept it all inside for years. When the police unearthed them, they were reluctant to come forward. Joe said that as a group they had addictions, relationship problems, anxiety, and brushes with the law. He was relieved that none of them was an abuser of children. He said that in all his life he had never met a group of people who had endured so much damage. I offered to see all of the young men for free on an ongoing basis. Only one came in.

Part III

Justice

28

Getting Ready to Go

Aaron

It was seven months from the time of Jerry's arrest to his trial in June 2012. In that time, I had a lot of random emotions hitting me at once. I was happy, upset, anxious. Most of all, I was anxious. I knew the trial meant more testimony from me in front of a new group of strangers. I told myself that I'd testified three times before, so this time it should be easier. The problem was, I still couldn't get past the part of me that worried nobody would believe me. I was also afraid that I would either freeze up when I took the stand or collapse the way I had before. I felt like I was on a roller coaster. The one thing that settled me down was that I knew I wasn't alone this time. There would be other guys there who were Jerry's victims.

Victim. I had a problem with that word.

Another thing bothered me: In the days before the trial, the news was still so much about Joe Paterno. He had died six months before, but everyone was still upset and angry that he had been fired. People were angry because he had such an amazing career and then it was taken from him so quickly and right before he died. At one time, Paterno was someone I admired, too. I even met him a couple of times when I was at the Second Mile and on the campus. He was a legend and, like a lot of people, I had put him on a high pedestal. When he fell off that pedestal, a part of me felt that I had started it all. But then I told myself that I was the first one to say something, and there were the others who might have stayed in hiding if it hadn't been for me coming forward. Mike said I should think of myself as a hero and not a victim. And even though I thought, *Wow, it's true—maybe I just saved a bunch of kids who could have been future victims*, and even though yes, I felt good about myself, when Paterno got fired I wasn't happy. I didn't feel like a hero. I liked Penn State football and I liked Paterno as a coach. But at the same time, it really threw me to think that he could have done something to stop what Jerry was doing years ago.

By the time the trial came around, I knew that a lot of people had been aware all along of what Jerry was doing and had done nothing to stop him. Like people at the Second Mile—maybe some of them weren't exactly aware of what was going on with Jerry, but I was certain that many of them knew something. I was also sure that many of them were suspicious and looked the other way. It made me angry. How could they not have said something to someone? If they even suspected something that was going on with just one kid, how could they pretend not to see, or erase in their minds what they knew existed?

I thought about teachers and principals who let me down and didn't take me seriously enough. The ones who didn't believe me or didn't want to believe me. They were the same ones who turned their eyes away when Jerry came to my school and took me out of classes. Like Coach Turchetta. Didn't he ever wonder what Jerry was doing? Didn't he want to ask him why? What would have been different if, just once, he'd asked Jerry why?

After Jerry's arrest, and for sure by the time of the trial, when everything was all over the news, a lot of my friends suspected that I was "Victim 1" and fell away from me. There were also the friends who stayed and were still very cool with me. I've learned a lot over the last few years when it comes to whom to trust and admire. I've learned a lot about who my friends are.

Mom and I left the house early in the morning for the state police barracks, where we met Mike before the trial. I showered and put on a pair of khaki pants, a yellow and orange button-down with the sleeves rolled up, and my loafers. I thought how I had to have the same kind of determination as I did when I ran track. I'd start out slow and hold my head high and then pick up the pace. I remembered what my distance coach taught me about running through pain.

I was as ready as I could be.

Mike

IT WAS ALMOST IMPOSSIBLE TO BELIEVE THAT THE TRIAL DATE WAS here. The pressure in the days before was excruciating in more ways than one. Not long before the trial, in May, my sister Sue died of a heart attack. It was out of the blue and left her husband, children, and the remaining three of us siblings in shock. We were still trying to recover from the loss of our brother. I wanted to be there for my nieces and nephew and yet I was consumed with this case. I had put my personal life on hold for Aaron. Some people might see it as a sacrifice, but it wasn't. It felt necessary. Even though I had dealt with victims of child sexual abuse for years, Aaron's case was the most ruthless I'd ever seen. And I've seen bad cases with children whose bones were broken and females who were raped by multiple perpetrators. Still, Aaron's was far worse because he was mentally manipulated and betrayed for so long during a critical stage in his development. I felt an enormous responsibility to make certain this broken boy didn't fall apart and also to put him back together. The care of Aaron nearly usurped time spent with my own children. And it wasn't because the perpetrator was Jerry Sandusky; it was because the perpetrator happened to be a powerful and well-connected man who could all too easily get away with it. I was hell-bent on not letting that happen.

June 15, 2011, was a warm, beautiful summer day—and yet it felt surreal. I took my shower, put on my suit and tie, packed up my briefcases filled with papers and notes, and hit the road.

It was about a forty-five-minute drive to the state police barracks. I didn't listen to any news stations as I drove to the courthouse. I knew that all the stations would be buzzing with Sandusky's trial and I didn't want to hear what anyone had to say. I wasn't interested in listening to all the editorializing and the predictions and the opinions. I put on the classic rock station on XM radio and cranked it loud. There were a string of songs by the Who and the Rolling Stones. Whenever I listen to music from my youth, I can remember where and when I first listened to it. Each song seems to hold some sort of significance for me. That day, there was one that held a new meaning. When they played the Who's "Behind Blue Eyes," even though I'd heard that song my whole life, I had never heard the lyric the way I did as I drove down Interstate 80 to the barracks.

No one knows what it's like . . .
And I blame you.

I thought back to when I was kid and first heard so many of those songs and life was so innocent. Now, here I was going to this trial—this incredible, national deal—and I was in the thick of it along with a boy whose life had accidentally fallen into my hands. Some thirty years before, back when I was in college, I never would have dreamed that something like this would happen. I remembered visiting Penn State when I was around eighteen or nineteen, just hanging out there with friends while we listened to our rock music with hardly a care in the world. I wondered how much of me was the same guy who put himself through college and grad school. I wanted to retain the ideals from my younger years, but I knew they'd been chipped away a little. I thought how much life had changed—my parents were gone, two of my siblings were gone, and whatever faith I had in our justice system had eroded in the last few years. As I drove, I felt an urgency to move on and to recapture what was lost. We needed to win this case. There had to be justice for Aaron and for the other boys who were abused by Sandusky—and for all the children out there who needed to be protected from predators like him. There was so much on the line as I drove through the mountains on Interstate 80.

My tension level was profound as I worried about Aaron. I wondered what he needed and if he was all right. I knew that he was being brave, determined not to let that stiff upper lip tremble, but I also knew that he was still hesitant and afraid. I had tried to bolster his spirits in the months before the trial. I reminded him how many boys he was saving going forward, repeating over and over that he wasn't just instrumental in bringing Sandusky's past victims out of the shadows, he was preventing this from happening to potential victims. If Sandusky remained at the Second Mile, if he hadn't been indicated by CYS years before when Aaron told his painful story, how many other children might have fallen prey to Sandusky? And going forward, how many countless others would there be?

On the day that Sandusky was arrested, if Aaron had his way, they would have put him in jail and thrown away the key. From the moment Aaron walked into CYS, and particularly after Sandusky's arrest, this trial loomed—alternately the most dreaded and anticipated day on Aaron's calendar. As my cellphone lay beside me in the car, I thought, *Please don't let it ring and be Dawn or an emergency room telling me that Aaron has had an anxiety attack that has landed him in the hospital again.*

Dawn and Aaron arrived at the barracks right after I did, and we were escorted to a small conference room. The barracks itself was a madhouse. I couldn't believe the crowds. The place was buzzing with the most intensely concentrated energy. There were victims and witnesses, and even though there wasn't supposed to be any mingling, there was, for the simple reason that the barracks was just too jam-packed to keep everyone away from each other. In the commotion, Aaron and one of the boys who had been at the aborted preliminary hearing recognized each other. Aaron went over to him and shook his hand and Dawn hugged him. That was the first time that Aaron and the boy said each other's names out loud, and in that moment there was a profound sense of liberation from the strange burden of the anonymous signature "victim," attached to a number. Aaron and this boy were the two primary witnesses, since the abuse they endured had been for the longest periods of time. With their secrecy momentarily lifted, an accidental bond was shared.

There were other familiar faces at the barracks as well. There was, once again, Scott Rossman, like a ghost from the past, and some other troopers whom I'd met before when I was at the barracks with McGettigan. Kelly, Jonelle, and Fina were already at the courthouse. There were a lot of plainclothes troopers from all over the state who were brought in for witness protection. Their job was to accompany witnesses and victims for the ten-minute drive to the courthouse in the county seat of Bellefonte. Just like it was at the preliminary hearing, the town of Bellefonte was shut down. The state police transported the witnesses in unmarked cars, vans, or SUVs—all with blacked-out windows. The main concern was avoiding an assault from the press as victims and witnesses entered the courthouse.

I hoped I wasn't overdoing it as a one-man rally around Aaron, repeating, "You're going to do great. Everyone is on your side now." He was nodding and saying, "I know," but I wasn't convinced of his certainty. I wasn't sure if he really believed that everyone was on his side. I just wanted to keep Aaron's spirits up.

I understood the process of jury selection known as voir dire, which means "to say what is true." Under the circumstances, the phrase was exceptionally compelling. Voir dire called for some standard questions requiring honesty: Do you have a personal connection to the case? Do you have any bias? How much do you think you know based upon public opinion? This case was all over the news, and the venue wasn't changed as it might have been in a similar situation where counsel felt either the plaintiff or defendant could be unjustly compromised by public opinion. It was also nerve-racking to know that the prosecution and defense each had the ability to reject a certain number of prospective jurors, of the roughly twenty citizens total, without having to give a specific reason. To think that a single group would determine the fate of this man I knew to be guilty.

After the selection, McGettigan admitted that we had a strong Penn State presence on the jury. There were employees, faculty, and alumni. How could we not? The courthouse was only ten miles from State College. This was Sandusky country. When Penn State people were chosen as jurors by Amendola, however, McGettigan did not exercise his right to object, and I wondered if that was wise. He insisted, however, that he had faith that the jury consisted of the right people despite their university affiliations. He felt that he had an ironclad case. McGettigan is a very wily coyote and the smartest guy in the room even though he comes off as a regular Joe. I was assured that he not only had a plan but in fact a carefully mapped-out strategy. But then I started thinking, *What if one, just one, of those jurors says this is a bunch of bullshit, and then we have a mistrial? What if, because of just one juror, everything we worked for goes down the toilet and we have to go through all of this again?* I didn't think Aaron could handle that at all. I wasn't sure if I could, either.

Dawn, Aaron, and I were transported separately, since I had to be in the courtroom earlier for my seat assignment. Two state troopers were assigned to me from the Pittsburgh jurisdiction, and with little warning, they rushed me from the barracks to

Bellefonte. Every access road was blocked by local police and sheriff's deputies. Each time we came to a roadblock, the troopers showed their badges to get passage. Security was even tighter than they anticipated, with a lot of blockades, and we were all worried that we might not get there on time for my designated seating.

The street was cordoned off with steel barriers but the media stood in a horseshoe shape just on the other side, ready to pounce. On the other side of the barriers, hundreds of media vehicles and people—satellite trucks, photographers, reporters—lined the narrow streets of Bellefonte. Finally, we pulled in around the back and drove up the steep hill to a white tent, which doubled as a corridor extending from the rear entrance of the courthouse, where I was escorted from the car and then whisked inside. Most of the courtroom gallery was filled with media. There was a lottery system to score seats, but even with the press presence inside, it was astounding how many media were outside and fighting to get past the barricades to the front lines.

A mid-nineteenth-century structure, the Bellefonte Courthouse anchors the center of town in an area known as the Diamond. The courtroom itself is small; close quarters are relieved only by the high ceilings hung with elaborate chandeliers. The windows are framed with red brocade draperies. It is staid and suggests simpler times. I doubted that courtroom had ever seen a trial like the one that was to come. For sure, the sleepy town of Bellefonte never expected an invasion such as this one.

Once inside the door, the troopers handed me over to the sheriff's deputies who were in charge of the interior and chaperoned me to the courtroom. They were young, fairly big guys in black uniforms—and not particularly polite. As a matter of fact, they were downright irritable and seemed aggravated that they had to deal with all the controlled chaos. Back at the barracks, I had heard from some of the troopers that cooperation from the sheriff's office with the state police had been poor as they tried to plan the transportation and security logistics surrounding the trial. I could definitely sense the friction that day. I think it was because of all the fallout on Penn State. We were, after all, in the lion's mouth. The state of Pennsylvania was prosecuting the case and here we all were in Bellefonte, a ten-minute drive from Penn State. Obviously, the sheriff and the deputies all knew Jerry Sandusky. He probably even gave some of them tickets to games at Beaver Stadium. For sure, a lot of those sheriffs and deputies had worked traffic detail when the cars were backed up for fifteen miles before a Penn State football game.

I took my seat on a bench with Jonelle, Linda Kelly, and a couple of other officials from the attorney general's office, directly behind Joe McGettigan and Frank Fina, who sat together at the prosecution desk.

During one of the breaks, a sheriff gave me a hard time when I came back up to take my seat. Even after I presented my ID from Clinton County, he questioned the credential. He didn't believe me when I said that I was there with the attorney general. Fortunately, there was a woman already seated who was watching this ridiculous display. She asked if I needed help and then called over to Jonelle, who told the sheriff to let me through. It was like we were the away team at a homecoming game.

29

Testimony

Aaron

When Mom and I got to the courthouse, the sheriff brought us to a back room where I waited to be called to the stand. I was only in the courtroom during my own testimony. None of the witnesses or the victims heard one another's testimony. Mom wasn't in the courtroom, because I didn't want her there. I still couldn't bear the thought of her listening to my story, even though she knew some of it at that point. I figured she guessed a lot of it as well, but I still wouldn't discuss it with her and I did not want her to know any details. In some ways, I guess I was protecting us both. I knew that Mom was frustrated because she couldn't be inside, but I said that having Mike in there and having her out there made me feel like I had a good tag team supporting me.

Joe McGettigan and Frank were seated directly across from the witness stand and Mike was sitting right behind them with Jonelle. To the left was the jury and to my right was the judge. At a diagonal to the judge, about nine feet from me, were the defense team and Jerry, who was sitting at a table with Amendola. Sarge and some other people sat behind them. It was weird being so close to Jerry. It shook me up. There was no way for me to avoid seeing him unless I looked straight ahead. McGettigan coached me to make eye contact with the judge and the jury, and because of where everyone was positioned and because the room was so tight, it seemed like Jerry was everywhere I looked. Even when I managed to avoid Jerry's eyes because my hands were over my own, at one point as I told my story, I could feel his stare go right through me.

Jerry actually smiled during my testimony. Every time I caught his eye, he had a grin on his face. It was crazy. When I answered a question on the stand that had to do with what Jerry did to me, his smile turned into a smirk, like he was shrugging off everything I said. He acted like he didn't care that he was on trial; he was letting me know that he'd get off scot-free because he was untouchable and no one was ever going to get him.

A part of me wanted to get up, walk over, and just hit him. Honestly, that's what I wished I could do. He was smiling as if to say that he was going to get away with it. I knew that he was trying to mess with my head. Even when he was on TV, after he was arrested, he was always smiling for the camera. I thought, *This is exactly what he did when I was a little boy.* He was acting like everything was all right when it wasn't, and he knew I'd never tell because who would believe my word against his?

Amendola's cross-examination felt like an attack. I like to think of myself as a cocky guy who won't put up with people who are all over me and trying to get in my face. Before all this happened with Jerry, I was like that for sure. I was a track star in high school and could confidently outrun anyone. I am protective, a real big brother when it comes to Bubby and Katie. But I knew that I couldn't be cocky on the stand. I just had to answer the questions and keep down my anxiety and anger, even though I was also embarrassed and humiliated. My testimony was only about a half hour but it felt like it lasted forever. Amendola was a guy I couldn't outrun.

At the end of the day, one of Jerry's victims came over to me and asked if we could speak alone. He looked like he was about ten years older than me. We went off to the side and then he apologized for not coming forward when "it" first happened to him years before with Jerry. He felt real bad and said that if he had spoken up at the time Jerry was abusing him, maybe it might not have happened to the rest of us. I told him that I understood why he couldn't come forward at the time. I said that I didn't want to say anything for the longest time. I even told him that if Jerry would have just left me alone when I said I didn't want to hang out with him anymore, instead of his acting like a clingy girlfriend and going crazy the way he did, I might not have said anything, either. What Jerry did to me and those other boys is the kind of stuff you just want to bury.

Dawn

MY OTHER CHILDREN KNEW WHAT HAPPENED TO THEIR BROTHER by the time the trial came around. Even though Katie is pretty fragile emotionally, I needed to be up front with her. I wanted her to know from me and not from someone else or from rumors. Bubby, as young as he is, had already figured out everything. I was shocked. He actually came up to me after Jerry was arrested and said that he thought that Jerry Sandusky molested Aaron. Bubby said that he heard kids talking in school about some kid in Lock Haven who had been sexually abused. When he saw Jerry's picture in the paper, he was positive that the boy they were now calling Victim 1 was his brother. I recalled the times that Jerry had been in our apartment and also the night that Jerry and Sarge babysat for Katie and Bubby. I asked Bubby if Jerry ever did anything to him and he said that he would have told me if he had.

When I waited for Aaron while he was on the stand, I kept thinking about all the reasons that I had been in such denial. I told myself over and over that it was because Jerry was who he was. It wasn't like Jerry was the strange guy who lives down the road and hangs out in the park. Jerry was the man everyone admired for his work with kids. My God, even my own father thought that Jerry was heaven-sent. Still, I was filled with regret. When Jerry came into my life and Aaron's, he was like a knight in shining armor, especially given what I'd been through—and yes, what I'd put myself through since I was seventeen. I really thought that Jerry could give Aaron what I couldn't afford and wasn't capable of doing for him. I truly thought that Jerry could get him into college. I believed the bill of goods he sold me when he took Aaron on trips to meet pro teams like the Philadelphia Eagles and things like that. I knew they stayed in hotels, but I thought there were other kids, and even when I heard that Jerry and Aaron shared a room, I assumed there were two beds, just like I have when I stay in a hotel room with my own kids. I trusted Jerry in the same way that I trust my own father. To this day, I'll sleep in the same room as my dad if we're in a hotel, and so would Aaron. I would never think there was anything wrong with that.

After all of this came out with Aaron, and as Jerry's other victims came forward, I was just so sad. I wondered how many more still hadn't spoken up. I was relieved that Jerry couldn't hurt any more boys. And to be perfectly honest, I also felt a sense of relief that I wasn't the only parent who had been fooled by Jerry Sandusky. Knowing that Jerry deceived other parents lifted my burden of feeling at fault, even if just ever so slightly. The fact that I fell for the deception haunted me, but knowing I wasn't the only parent who fell for Jerry's con made me feel less gullible. Jerry was too cunning for all of us—not just me.

I still don't know how to answer those people who condemn me for not seeing what they say was right before my eyes. The ones who anger me, though, are those who say I "allowed" this to happen. I suppose the only thing I can say is that this could happen to anyone. When someone acts like a savior, you don't question their intentions. I learned the hard way that you always should, though. Perhaps if Aaron had gone off with some other teacher or a coach, I might have looked at the situation differently, because that person wouldn't have had the golden reputation that Jerry had. Who would have thought in a million years that Jerry would abuse all those children? How could he pull the wool over so many people's eyes? Yet he did.

I am proud of my son, though it pains me to think about what he went through. I wasn't sure how he would bear up through the trial. I was told he did well on the stand. A part of me felt rejected when he said that he didn't want me in the courtroom, but I understood his reasons.

At least, once Aaron's truth came out, we all kept pushing. Yes, it was after the fact but at least I pushed along with Mike and we went into high gear. And in the end, we exposed Jerry as the traitor he was. He not only abused my child, he abused my trust, our family, the community, and other innocent children. Hindsight is always 20/20.

Mike

WHEN AMENDOLA CROSS-EXAMINED AARON, HE WAS BRUTAL. HE employed the old courtroom tactic of asking the same question over and over again in slightly different ways to try to unnerve and fluster the witness. He did this to the other victims as well. I was hoping that objections would be raised but I remembered what McGettigan said when I questioned him about protecting Aaron on the stand. He said that sometimes it's better not to object and to let someone like Amendola simply show themselves for who they are. In addition, McGettigan said that frequent objections too often result in text that's struck from the records and is therefore not considered by the jurors—and often that omitted text can be key when it comes to scrutinizing both the facts and nuance of the case. The jury reads transcripts from both sides and McGettigan was certain that the jury would know what's what. He actually *wanted* Amendola to show his true colors. As I watched the assault on Aaron, I wished McGettigan's confidence was contagious.

Amendola tried every which way to agitate and confuse Aaron. One specific sequence stands out in my memory: He asked if Aaron ever talked to anyone, including his mother, about getting money because of the accusations he made against Jerry Sandusky. I wondered if Amendola was implying extortion. When Aaron replied "no," Amendola asked the question again, just slightly differently: Is that why you're here today, because you want to make money? Again Aaron said no. Amendola persisted in asking if Aaron ever said anything to a neighbor about getting money from this. No again. And then, isn't it true you're planning to buy a new Jeep when this is all over, if you should win the case? No. Amendola was pounding Aaron. It was like listening to dirty cops beating a confession out of an innocent suspect; my worry was that sometimes that innocent suspect finally admits guilt just so the cops will stop.

Amendola had to know how desperate Aaron was for him to stop, and I'm certain that he hoped Aaron would finally just cave. His ruthlessness was his way of letting Aaron know that he would only stop once Aaron "cried uncle" and said the accusations were false and retracted them. Aaron remained strong and steadfast, but I could see that he was becoming increasingly upset and hesitant to respond.

At one point, Aaron looked directly at me and mouthed, "Please make him stop."

I can't begin to explain how my heart broke when he mouthed those words. I wanted to stand up and say that *I* objected, even though McGettigan was letting Amendola carry on and banking that Aaron would stay the course. It was like I was outside my body. I had to stop myself, holding back what felt almost like a reflex to scream, "I object!" Aaron looked so sad and earnest and there were Amendola's piercing eyes and I felt so helpless. All I could do was just nod my head at Aaron ever so slightly and hold my hands firm and parallel to one another about a foot apart. I was using sign language. *Hold steady and hang on. It's almost over.*

After Aaron's testimony, Dawn and Aaron were escorted back to the barracks and Dawn drove Aaron back home. I had to keep my seat in the courtroom until it adjourned for the day. I called Aaron from my car on the way home. He was relieved that the testimony was over. He was also proud of himself for taking the stand, and not breaking under Amendola's fire. But he was still scared that the jury would not convict Sandusky.

The proceedings went on for one week. I stayed for a few days to hear major testimony from other victims and witnesses. Even though my presence wasn't mandatory, I wanted to be there. I needed to hear what the other victims said about Sandusky. I wanted to hear details about the serialized pattern of behavior that I suspected from the beginning—long before I knew who Sandusky was and when I just knew from Aaron's sordid and heartbreaking tale that his experience could not have been one isolated case.

I made certain to be there for McGettigan's closing argument. He asked the jury to consider the lives of the group of victims as they considered the verdict and to find Sandusky guilty of everything. McGettigan's words were chilling when he referred to the victims as "ten broken souls."

30

The Verdict

Mike

As the jury deliberated, I was obligated to attend the Pennsylvania Psychological Association convention at the Hilton in Harrisburg—right in Strawberry Square and right near the attorney general's office. The site was all too coincidental. The association was presenting me with an award titled "Psychology in the Media," which recognized a body of work in connection with the media for the last fifteen years. The award was decided long before anyone knew about the Sandusky case and my involvement, and now it seemed ironic that the media constituted an entity that I had to elude.

I was torn as to whether or not to go, but long before this trial was on the horizon, I had promised my seventeen-year-old daughter that we would go together. She was proud and excited for me and I didn't want to disappoint her. But really, I wanted to be at the courthouse waiting for the verdict.

Maybe it was my imagination, but when I arrived at the Hilton, I felt that some of my colleagues were treating me strangely. I had a feeling that a lot of them were either angry or sad—or, perhaps, both—about the ignominious fall of Penn State football and the disgrace levied upon their beloved JoePa. Despite the award, I felt like persona non grata—and knew that I wasn't mistaken. Just after Sandusky's arrest back in November, one of the psychologists in the association sent out a message to the members asking them to support me since I was instrumental in Sandusky's arrest. It generated neither support nor congratulations. Rather, it generated little response except from one psychologist who wrote to me. "I just lost my faith in humanity. JoePa was my idol." It all went back to Paterno and Penn State despite the victims and regardless of what Sandusky had done.

My daughter and I went home after the ceremony. I was toying with the idea of cruising down to the courthouse and just hanging around while the jurors deliberated. I opted not to go. Everyone's best guess was that there wouldn't be a verdict until at least the end of the weekend. Aaron had just started his first real job, as a security guard, and he was working the graveyard shift that night. By nine thirty, we all figured that the jury had retired for the evening. The three of us—Dawn, Aaron, and I—were in constant communication that night, calling and texting.

I figured that in the unlikely event that a verdict came back that night, McGettigan or someone from the attorney general's office would call in plenty of time for me to run and pick up Dawn and Aaron so we could all head over to the courthouse. There were no calls and nothing seemed to be happening when Aaron left for work around ten. Dawn was watching the news at her place and I was in my living room with the TV news playing in the background, the volume on low. I was barely paying attention. Then Dawn called: The jury was coming back. I turned up the TV and there was the breaking news. Dawn and I debated whether we should meet down in Bellefonte, but then the newsman said the verdict was expected within twenty minutes. We knew that Bellefonte was shut down to everyone except for the press and officials. Even if we sped over there, the roads were closed and we wouldn't even get a parking spot within miles of the courthouse. We never expected that jury verdict to come in that night.

We stayed on the phone, glued to the television. The jury deliberated for twenty-one hours after hearing a week of testimony from ten victims. We were silent as the verdict was announced: The jury found Jerry Sandusky guilty on 45 of 48 counts of child sexual abuse, which could result in a possible maximum of 442 years in prison. Based upon the jury's findings, the abuse had gone on since 1997, when Sandusky was fifty-one years old—two years before Sandusky "retired" as assistant football coach at Penn State.

Dawn must have repeated the phrase "Thank God, it's over" a million times, and then she called Aaron, who was on the road and had to pull over because he was crying so much when he heard the news, he couldn't see to drive.

June 22, 2012, was the date stamped on the reward given to me that morning—and the date that the guilty verdict in the trial of Jerry Sandusky was decided. At last, it was over.

But it wasn't over for the victims and probably never would be, even though Aaron and all the other victims got the justice they deserved. Of course, for me, it was more about Aaron than anyone else. I thought about how this manipulative son of a bitch Sandusky played games right to the end. Such hubris that he never even took the stand. All along, he thought that he was above the law. But now, finally, Aaron had used the law to take the monster down.

Epilogue

Mike

ON THE DAY AFTER THE VERDICT, AARON AND I MET IN MY LOCK Haven office. We hugged—a "guy hug" that lasted a second, which was the closest we ever came to an embrace. Except for his girlfriend, Aaron still doesn't like to be touched.

Now it's over, and yet I still have trouble sleeping. My insomnia started about six months after I first met Aaron and it continues to this day. I'm not sure if I'll ever stop thinking about Aaron's case.

One Saturday in August, about a month and a half after the verdict was returned, I took an early morning drive with a definite destination and a few planned detours along the way. I wanted to revisit familiar places. I wanted to visit those I'd only seen in photographs at the trial. I wanted to visit some I had merely imagined in my mind's eye.

It was a sunny, cloudless days with a perfect turquoise sky. The highway, flanked on either side by the profile of the Nittany Mountains and endless pastures, cuts through beautiful country. Long ago cougars roamed those mountains, and recently I read that those cougars—a species also known as Nittany lions—had suddenly been seen again. I wondered if they were really making a comeback or if this was yet another legend waiting to be debunked.

My first stop was Bellefonte. The steep hill on the street leading to the rear entrance where we were covertly escorted through the tent and past the steel barricades was now returned to unoccupied territory. The barricades were gone; the media had retreated. The courthouse in Diamond Square could not have looked more staid, its scrolled Ionic columns symbolizing strength, surrounded by potted plants with blossoming red and yellow flowers. In the square, there was a wrought-iron bench and an old-fashioned water fountain evocative of simpler times. The businesses housed in Victorian buildings and the small private homes with their front porches lining the streets were restored to tranquility. The trial of Jerry Sandusky would forever alter the town's history, but the perceptible debris was swept away.

From Bellefonte, I took Interstate 99 southwest and headed to State College. On the right, in low-lying land marked only by an American flag, was the Centre County Correctional Facility: the temporary home of Jerry Sandusky until he is moved to a permanent state prison. I thought how fitting it was that on a clear day like this, Sandusky could probably see Beaver Stadium only six miles away as he stood in the prison yard.

It had been several years since I was on the Penn State campus. As I drove inside the gates, the grounds were lush and green. I envisioned summers at the Second Mile, and the children who otherwise would have spent days such as this one playing in concrete schoolyards. Here was a world filled with manicured playing fields, all kinds of sporting equipment at their fingertips, and yet it was a false paradise for far too many of them.

I walked the main street of the campus and noted the high-end clothing shops, the playhouse, the bookstores, several jewelers, and I had no question as to why the area was dubbed the Happy Valley. It was surely an Eden before the fall and I wondered how long it would be until all of this was forgotten and drifted back into the manicured landscape. I came to a shop filled with Penn State souvenirs—one of which was a newly created T-shirt printed on the front with "NCAA" but the "C" was, instead, a hammer and sickle. Underneath the logo, it read "National Communist Athletic Association." On the back it read "Overstepping their bounds and punishing the innocent since 1906." The shirt was not university-approved, but I can't say that I disagreed with the content.

After the "greatest scandal in the history of sports," as it came to be known, the school was punished by the NCAA with unprecedented sanctions against the football program and a $60 million fine levied against the university—an endowment to be established and used around the nation to serve victims of child abuse. Penn State players were banned from bowl games and postseason for four years; scholarships were reduced from twenty-five to fifteen annually; returning athletes were unable to transfer and immediately compete; the football program itself was on a five-year probation; the NCAA would vacate all wins of the Nittany Lions football team from 1998 to 2011. I have a problem with a lot of that. Yes, fine the university and make it pay, but why punish the players and students who were innocents in all this? As for the NCAA's right to investigate and impose sanctions on individuals—I agree with that, but it should have happened years ago, when everyone knew but turned a blind eye.

My next stop was the "Pattee Library and Paterno Library." There was Joe Paterno's name carved in stone. JoePa's statue had already been removed from Beaver Stadium but the library would keep his name. The library was dedicated in 1997 with fundraising efforts by Paterno and his wife, Sue. JoePa once said that you can't have a great university without a great library. That's the kind of guy we thought he was.

I got back in my car and drove down College Avenue for about three miles. If I made a left turn, I would drive right into

Beaver Stadium, which was across from the turn I made instead onto Grandview Avenue, where Sandusky lived. I was struck by the fact that Sandusky's little private Idaho was exactly between the county correctional facility and the Penn State campus.

Grandview is windy and narrow and forks at one point, where you can take either an upper or lower road. I wasn't sure which way to go, but I took the low one. A sign informed me there was no outlet; another advised to slow down for children. Although I'd seen the house in photographs, this was quite different. Sandusky's house stood at the end of the cul-de-sac. Two cars, sporting Penn State vanity plates, were parked in the driveway outside the two-car garage. The house is pink and brown, appearing to be gingerbread, with a pristine green velvet lawn rolling down the front yard. It could have been a painting in a child's storybook. The house looked like the safest place in the world, nestled in this quintessential suburban neighborhood. I stared at it for quite a while thinking about that windowless basement room in its bowels. When I looked up, I saw—not thirty feet beyond the fence of Sandusky's backyard—the tops of playground equipment for the district's elementary school.

A shudder went up my spine. I got back in my car to leave and had difficulty turning around on that tight dead end. I didn't want to back into anyone's driveway or onto a neighbor's lawn. That was when I noticed the signs stuck into the ground of two homes on either side of Sandusky's. At first I thought they were "For Sale" signs, and figured, *Wow, people no longer wanted to live on a street that was the scene of horrific crimes.* But as I looked closer, I saw that the signs were sponsored by RAINN, the Rape, Abuse & Incest National Network. Across the top they read, "Support Victims of Sexual Abuse." There was poetry in that.

————

Aaron

IT'S FINALLY OVER. AT LEAST THE TRIAL IS OVER AND JERRY Sandusky will never see freedom again. Now the other victims and I have to fight for *our* freedom. I know there's a long road ahead of me.

Am I recognizable? Everyone in my town knows who I am because I ran track for the high school and represented my school in the States Competition. A lot of times, my picture was in the town paper on the front page of the sports section. Now, when I'm running around town and practicing, someone always stops and waves and calls out, "How's it going, Aaron?" So, people know me as a runner, and although no one has come right out and asked me, I think they also know "who" I am in terms of Jerry Sandusky. Lock Haven is a small town. There's talk about the most minor stuff, like what this neighbor is doing and who said what to whom. But this case was big talk. After the verdict came in, a teacher came up to me and shook my hand. He said that I was a hero for doing what I did. He didn't go into any details or name names, but there was this silent understanding. I knew what he was congratulating me for and it wasn't for running track. I just walked away and said thanks because I didn't want him to see me cry.

I don't want people ever to see me cry and I don't want people to feel sorry for me.

So, am I recognizable? Yes. But the only thing that really matters is if I'm recognizable to *me*—because for a long time, I wasn't.

I want kids and adults to know that this can happen regardless of who you are or where you live. Whether it's a big city or a small town, whether you're a track star like me or not, whether it's a guy like Jerry or the guy next door—*this can happen*. There are way too many people out there like Jerry Sandusky who will try to get into a little kid's life. I'm not saying that kids shouldn't trust people, but I am saying that they need to look around and keep a guard up.

I want to hit the road with Mike and talk to kids and parents and teachers. It's really important for parents to tell kids, remind them all the time, that if they ever feel strange vibes from someone, it's okay to say so. There can be no shame or embarrassment in speaking up. It's important for adults to let kids know that they can. Parents have got to have intuition about this kind of thing. And if parents feel a vibe from another adult, they have to speak up as well.

It's true that kids need to be trusted by their parents, but kids need to trust their parents too. Even if the parent is the type like my mom, who lets you be totally independent and trusts you completely, as a kid you have to know you can go to your parent and they'll be there to help you. Parents need to let their kids know that they're not alone out there. I want children and parents to feel empowered when it comes to this, because it exists.

Even though something bad like this happened to me, I will not hold back on what I want to do. Yes, I wish that someone had intervened and done more for me so it wouldn't have happened at all, but I have to let that go. Did Jerry Sandusky steal years of my life? He did. But I am moving forward. I will not wallow in self-pity. Do I think that maybe I "shoulda coulda woulda" done what I've told Mike a million times and just pushed Jerry away from me and run from his house screaming? Yes, I wish I had. But the thing is, I was just eleven when it started and a little kid doesn't have that kind of courage. At almost fifteen, it was finally a different story. But I want to make sure that even the littlest kid has the courage to run from an adult like Jerry.

Right now, I want to go to college. I'm being followed by a lot of schools for track scholarships and there's one that's my favorite. For the obvious reasons, a lot of things got put on hold—like my SATs. I still have to take those but they're only given twice a year, in spring and fall. Fall was the arrest and spring was the

Aaron and Dawn celebrate his graduation from
Sugar Valley Rural Charter School

trial. Like I said, obvious reasons. There's also a lot of paperwork and applications that I have to get in order. Back in ninth grade, my grades slipped because of all this, but toward the end of my senior year, I came close to making the honor roll after I switched to the new school. I'm still thinking about being a state trooper, and even though you don't have to go to college for that, they prefer it—and I want an education. I have no doubts about passing the physical test easily for trooper and maybe I could even ace the written one, but I really want to go to college and study criminal justice with a focus in law. If the college I like doesn't have a law focus in criminal justice, then I want to major in history. If it doesn't work out with the state troopers, then I want to teach history. I have a lot of plans, backup plans, and dreams. And I'm going to chase my dreams, and all the nightmares be damned.

I am not a victim. Not anymore.

Afterword

Mike

Neuroscience has yet to unearth the reason and cause for pedophilia. The American Psychiatric Association's *Diagnostic and Statistical Manual of Mental Disorders* (DSM-IV) defines pedophilia as recurrent sexually arousing fantasies, impulsive desires, and/or behaviors involving sexual acts with a child. Although studies of the pedophile's brain in the form of magnetic resonance imaging (MRI) and positron emission tomography (PET) scans have revealed certain abnormalities in the frontal and central regions, there is nothing conclusive from an organic point of view. Not only do many variables exist within each individual, but neuroscientists, psychiatrists, and psychologists differ among themselves as to the veracity and certainty of medical diagnoses as far as organic, forensic, and behavioral connections.

What we do agree upon is that pedophiles and serial child molesters blend well into society and come from all walks of life. This alone muddies the waters in terms of sociological, psychological, and medical profiles. We also know that 90 percent of victims are more than familiar with their abusers, who are usually adult males or male teenagers, presenting under the guise of fathers, brothers, neighbors, teachers, family friends . . . the list goes on. We state male abusers because although women also sexually abuse children, the occurrence is rare.

There are other firm statistics. For instance, often the abuser is a past victim of child molestation as well, and if so, seeks out children of the age he was when victimized.

But in other ways, the findings are inconsistent. If he is a teenager, he often presents as one of the "cool kids on the block." If an adult male, he is often married, responsible, well liked, respected, educated, and somewhat religious. He also enjoys being surrounded by children. Or the pedophile can be someone who appears to be socially awkward or somewhat maladjusted. In other words, there is no textbook profile. The "creepy" guy who likes to sit and watch kids in the playground may just be a harmless misfit, but the father pushing his own child on a swing may be a pedophile.

It is clear from both law enforcement investigative interviews and therapy sessions that pedophiles do not consider the welfare or the feelings of others—in particular, the helpless child. The pedophile's goal is to take total control and render the recipient powerless as they derive their own pleasure. In my opinion, throughout my more than twenty-five years of work with both abusers and their victims, it appears something is clearly missing in the superego or the conscience of the pedophile. Unfortunately, that "something" is yet to be identified.

I believe that a person is born with this proclivity and that when it comes to the victim, the only "cure" right now is prevention and intervention. The prevention of child sexual abuse and other forms of sexual coercion has been a public health concern for decades, its roots traceable to the nineteenth century, yet few validated prevention programs exist.

Just after Jerry Sandusky was arrested, I got a call from a man named Peter S. Pelullo, who had seen my name in the press. At first, I was cautious. There were a lot of callers who came out of the woodwork—some of whom were credible and others who were jumping on a tragic bandwagon. I even got a call from a female former Penn State secretary who said she was fired some twenty years before—and she was convinced it was because she reported seeing Sandusky taking little boys into the dormitory. I turned that case over to state police and the attorney general's office for further investigation. Pete told me about his recently established foundation, Let Go . . . Let Peace Come In (LGLPCI), an international outreach program directed at bringing adult men and women who were victims of child abuse to the recovery process. He explained that the foundation did not stand alone but, in fact, was aligned with the Johns Hopkins Bloomberg School of Public Health and had the goal of preventing child sexual abuse and the harm and suffering it inflicts, as well as improving treatment programs for adult survivors.

Pete asked me to come on board, not only to give professional advice on matters concerning mental health care for survivors, but to help disseminate information and educate. He also told me that he had recently published a book, *Betrayal and the Beast: A True Story of One Man's Journey Through Childhood Sexual Abuse, Sexual Addiction, and Recovery.* The book was Pete's autobiography.

Pete was the founder of Philly World Records and the owner of a premier recording studio in the 1970s; he worked with musicians like the Rolling Stones, Evelyn "Champagne" King, Harold Melvin and the Blue Notes, Cashmere, and Eugene Wilde. A native of Philadelphia and one of six children from a stable family (his parents' marriage lasted fifty-six years, until his father's death in 2004), Pete is sixty years old, married, and the father of two sons. Throughout his life, he presented to the outside world an image of professional and financial success, as well as domestic stability. Yet he harbored a dark secret that took forty-eight years to exhume as he battled a habit of sexual addiction.

In Pete's self-described "Ozzie and Harriet" neighborhood, there was a teenage boy named "John" who was a "cool" mentor as he babysat for seven-year-old Pete, who wanted to grow up to be just like him. Once John gained Pete's trust, he and his friend "Jimmy" repeatedly raped Pete over the course of several months. Jimmy's mother was a friend of Pete's mother, and Pete was not only afraid to ruin their friendship; under the threat of John and Jimmy, he was also afraid of retribution. After the publication of Pete's book, more boys from Pete's old neighborhood—now adult men—came forward to admit that they, too, had been abused by these neighborhood boys.

It is all too familiar a story.

Because neuroscience has yet to define medical/psychiatric reasons for this behavioral abnormality, one of the reasons that the LGLPCI foundation intrigued me was their wise alignment with Johns Hopkins Bloomberg School of Public Health. Child sexual abuse is a global public health problem and can no longer be considered a taboo that societies are reluctant to address. What is termed the Good Behavior Game came out of the Bloomberg Department of Mental Health more than twenty years ago. Targeting first- and second-grade children with an intervention by teachers to improve classroom behavior and reduce aggression, data are now being collected and analyzed in order to determine whether early intervention influences later adult sexual offending behaviors.

The research continues in the hope that as a global society we can *prevent* abuse before it happens rather than dealing with it after the fact, when a sex offender merely registers. Sadly, it has been found that registering as an offender has been of little use and effectiveness. The compulsive and impulsive nature of the pedophile's disorder does not dissuade the registered offender from abusing again—despite the court order. He may merely change the venue for his hunting ground, and slip through the cracks of a system where, although he is required to register, he does not. It is comparable to the ineffectiveness of a restraining order: How many times do we hear that an abusive boyfriend or husband has been found guilty of murder despite the restraining order in place?

Aaron and I are now both on board with Pete. Although Aaron is determined to attend college, he is equally as determined to be a spokesperson, in the hope that what happened to him will one day become extinct. We all agree that efforts must take place on grassroots levels, beginning with all-level schools across the country. Educating children, parents, teachers, and youth officers in law enforcement about the prevalence of this health issue is essential when it comes to prevention and intervention.

We want kids to know that if they are abused, it's nothing to be ashamed of and not their fault. We want children to come forward so they can get help before it's too late, and so that the abuser can be punished as well as removed. We want parents, teachers, and law enforcement to note the signs, have a full awareness of the grooming behavior in the pedophile, and respond to their own instincts. We will urge both children and adults to take responsible measures if and when they suspect that an adult is an abuser—regardless of that adult's stature in their community.

The obvious question that arises is one of trust. Aaron said it best: Parents have to trust their kids, but kids also have to trust their parents. As we go into the schools, we're not teaching kids *not to trust*, but rather *how and whom to trust*. We will also educate adults and children about abnormal sexuality, developing programs where adults and children can readily and shamelessly identify potential perpetrators.

We hope that the program will also encourage young active and potential pedophiles to seek help for what they can now identify as abnormal urges. Not only must the stigma of a victim's reporting a crime of sexual abuse be removed, but the stigma of carrying the hallmarks of pedophilia as a teenager must be recognized and removed as well. Anger and sexual addiction rehabilitation programs have been mainstreamed into the psychological and social arenas. The same must happen for those who conceal what they know are abnormal sexual feelings toward a child. In other words, the forums have to open in a way that invites acceptable conversation when it comes to sexual abuse. The taboo must be removed.

There can no longer exist what is termed "the bystander effect" or Genovese syndrome, where individuals do not offer assistance to a victim of a crime when other witnesses are present. There can no longer be the assumption that "someone else," another witness, will assume responsibility for intervention or a call for help. This psychological terminology was coined in 1968 by social psychologists John Darley and Bibb Latané following the 1964 murder of twenty-eight-year-old Kitty Genovese. Thirty-eight people watched from their windows as Kitty was stabbed to death near her home in a residential housing apartment complex in Kew Gardens, Queens, New York. Since that time, we have learned that, in fact, people *did* try to help but were paralyzed as the deadly attack took place before their eyes. This bystander effect, also known as diffusion of responsibility, remains in the jargon. This was also the case with those who suspected—and those who knew for a fact—that Jerry Sandusky was an abuser. Whether it was born out of a fear of losing a job, merely sullying the reputation of an institution or an individual, or compromising their own political aspirations, people left the responsibility to someone else. No one came forward—until there was Aaron.

The statistics are staggering. One in three girls and one in four boys are sexually abused before the age of eighteen. There are currently more than 60 million adult survivors of child abuse in the United States. If that many *survivors* have been documented and entered into the database, how many still have not come forward and continue to live silently with their pain? Data tell us that more than eight hundred children are sexually abused in the United States every day. Again, keep in mind that those statistics are only gathered from those who tell.

Furthermore, although length of time and depth of the abuse is a factor when it comes to the post-traumatic stress of the child, even if the abuse is only a single episode, the child is affected in one way or another and by varying degrees by that sexual exploitation. The effect continues well into his or her adult life. Left untreated, the trauma shapes the child's adult behavior, which is all too often laced with lifelong challenges—among them anxiety, depression, schizophrenia, bipolar disorder, drug and alcohol abuse, and sex addiction. Surprisingly, children of sexual abuse often lack physical evidence, which compromises their credibility both with themselves and criminal investigators: All too often the physical signs of trauma have healed by the time they come forward—and children tend to physically heal quickly. Even adolescent girls who were raped and subsequently become pregnant often do not present with medical evidence of trauma. Emotional signs of trauma, however, can remain locked within the victim's psyche as they search for the magic bullet to mask their pain.

In Aaron's case, and in the cases of Jerry Sandusky's other victims who came forward, we pulled off a miracle, and yet I still believe we've only just scratched the surface. Yes, Sandusky has been removed from society, but he is only one offender in an endless and murky sea of others—some of whom hold a similar stature and reputation to his and others who are more ordinary men with less political power. Again, the pedophile's identity has no distinct fingerprint.

If not for Aaron's courage to come forward, Jerry Sandusky might never have been revealed as the serial pedophile that he was. Despite his trauma, Aaron persisted for nearly three years as he waged battle against his offender. He fought a bureaucracy that was all but allowing this crime to be swept under the rug. He rallied despite overwhelming panic attacks as his hopes for an arrest were repeatedly shattered. He endured constant disappointment resulting from false promises for swifter justice. He struggled with debilitating symptoms resulting from conversion disorder as he was forced to tell his agonizing story all too many times while at the same time he felt that his credibility was questioned.

Despite the unwavering support of his mother and my counseling, justice for Aaron, and for the other victims who then garnered the courage to come forward as Aaron led the way, would not have happened if not for Aaron's tenacity and strength. If not for Aaron, Jerry Sandusky might still be in the Happy Valley plucking small boys from his stable of potential victims at the Second Mile, just as a sadist plucks the wings from butterflies. In my heart, I know that if Aaron's had been the only case for which Sandusky was found guilty, Sandusky would have received a slap on the wrist, perhaps given a five-year sentence with probation and issued a restraining order mandating that he stay away from children—and I am convinced that he still would have carried on the abuse under the radar. I also know that if Aaron's had been the only case and had he not been the incentive for the other victims to come forward, a "lack of evidence" would have prevailed, since one small boy against the likes of Sandusky would not have been enough.

But Aaron did come forward, and he never gave up until Sandusky's fate was sealed. Although he refutes the moniker, Aaron is most certainly a hero.

Acknowledgments

Although we wish that this book never had to be written, it did, and there are many people to thank. In order of appearance:

Our deep appreciation to Children and Youth Services: Clinton County Director Gerald Rosamilia, Assistant Director Jennifer Sobjak, Intake Officer Jessica Dershem, and Clinton County Commissioner Joel Long.

Our heartfelt gratitude goes to those in the State of Pennsylvania's Attorney General's Office: Attorney General Linda Kelly, Senior Deputy Attorney General Jonelle Eshbach, and Agent Anthony Sassano. Our thanks also to Pennsylvania State Trooper Corporal Scott Rossman and countless other agents and troopers who assisted with the investigation and prosecution of this case.

Our gratitude to RoseMarie Terenzio at RMT PR Management for believing in the importance of this story, bringing this project to light, and getting the word out there on our behalf; to our literary agent, Steve Troha at Folio Literary Management, for believing in us and in this book, and for handling the topic with sensitivity; to Steve's assistant, Nikki Thean, who skillfully helped us to write the proposal; and to Santina Leuci at ABC.

Thanks to literary agent Marcy Posner at Folio, who brought

us to our professional writer, Stephanie Gertler, whose exceptional abilities to accurately perceive and convey our thoughts and feelings proved invaluable.

Thank you to the people at Ballantine Books: Gina Centrello, president and publisher, The Random House Publishing Group; Elizabeth McGuire, publisher of Ballantine Bantam Dell; Susan Corcoran, director of publicity, Ballantine Bantam Dell; our tireless, ardent, and dedicated editor, Mark Tavani; and everyone at Ballantine in design, promotion, and sales who made this book a reality.

And finally, we are eternally indebted and grateful to Deputy Attorney General Joe McGettigan for fighting to the finish—and winning.

Dawn thanks those who supported her throughout and after this ordeal: her friends Jessica Heichel, Kathy Marr, Maryanne and Ralph Bergin, Erin Rutt Winslow; her parents, Donald and Sandy Fisher; her sister, Sheila Herman; and her fiancé, Steve Hennessey.

Aaron thanks his mother, Dawn Daniels, for her love and support; his former coach, Thom Hunter; and above all Mike Gillum, who saw him through the darkest days and brought him into the light.

Mike is grateful to his late parents, Dorothy Ann Gillum and Charles L. Gillum; his late sister, Susan Werth; and his late brother, Dr. Harold Gillum, who are all forever in his heart. He also thanks his sister, Jamie Hildreth, and brother, Dr. Charlie Gillum, for being there; his son, Austin, and daughter, Chloe, for all the time they allowed Mike to spend away from them; and his wife, Tina, for understanding once the story was revealed. Mike thanks Peter S. Pelullo at LGLPCI Foundation, who called at just the right time and gave faith in going forward. He is also grateful to his dear friend Adam Sedlock, who always stood by with compassion; the staff at the Pennsylvania Psychological Association, particularly Sam Knapp and Marti Evans, for their support and assistance; and his private office manager, Amy Woodley, for her endless transcriptions.

Aaron, Dawn, and Mike also thank those who sent cards and letters of support and, of course, the young men who had the courage to come forward in spite of their pain.

About the Authors

AARON FISHER plans to attend college after high school and someday become a Pennsylvania state trooper. Along with Mike Gillum, Aaron intends to tour various schools on behalf of the Let Go . . . Let Peace Come In Foundation, helping to educate children, teachers, and parents about the nature of child sexual abuse and its prevention. He lives in Pennsylvania.

MICHAEL GILLUM, M.A., is a licensed psychologist and a specialist in child abuse, sexual abuse, and other criminal behavior. The recipient of the Pennsylvania Psychological Association's 2012 Psychology in the Media Award, he offers his expertise as a consultant throughout the state for law enforcement, county courts, school districts, and human service agencies, including Children and Youth Services. He is on the board of directors of the Let Go . . . Let Peace Come In Foundation, which supports victims of child sexual abuse. He lives with his wife and children in Pennsylvania.

DAWN DANIELS is a fundraiser in her school district, working with local sports teams and cheerleading squads. She lives in Pennsylvania with her three children.